T0390442

Praise for Ashley Craft's
The Unofficial Disney Parks Drink Recipe Book

"If your mind was boggled and your taste buds blown by the sheer creativity, gorgeous photos, and just plain entertaining history and food facts of *The Unofficial Disney Parks Cookbook*, then you will be no less blown away by Ashley Craft's follow-up, *The Unofficial Disney Parks Drink Recipe Book*. From refreshing (Strawberry Acqua Fresca) to unusual (Blurrgfire) to comforting (Black Spire Hot Chocolate) to decadent (Brooklyn Blackout), these drinks evoke the magic and fun of the Disney Parks for young and old and everyone in between. Excuse me while I go into my kitchen to whip up some Frozen Sunshine."

—Dinah Bucholz, author of the *New York Times* bestseller
The Unofficial Harry Potter Cookbook

"What EVERY Disney fan needs in their life...seriously magic!"
—*Domestic Geek Girl*

"A drink here for everyone in the family."
—*The Disney Food Blog*

"There is something for everyone here."
—*The Game of Nerds*

Praise for Ashley Craft's
The Unofficial Disney Parks Cookbook

"The perfect gift to give your Disney-loving foodie friends for the holidays."
—*Elite Daily*

"Brings the magic of Disney Parks right to your home...Disney magic and a full belly, does it get better than that?"
—*Laughing Place*

"Just as good as being there."
—Today.com

Praise for Ashley Craft's
The Unofficial Disney Parks Cookbook

"Sure to satisfy anyone's Disney park cravings....Will make your family and friends' dreams come true."

—Reader's Digest

"Obsessed!"

—US Weekly

"Amazing!!"

—Disabled Disney

"Like taking a trip without leaving the house."

—Men's Journal

"Fantastic!"

—1StopMom

"Helps keep the magic alive."

—Better

"Better than a FastPass."

—BuzzFeed

"Will transport you directly into Disneyland."

—Business Insider

"A must for Disney foodies."

—Red Tricycle

The Unofficial Disney Parks EPCOT Cookbook

From **SCHOOL BREAD** in Norway to
MACARON ICE CREAM SANDWICHES in France,
100 EPCOT-Inspired Recipes for Eating and Drinking Around the World

ASHLEY CRAFT

Author of the *USA TODAY* Bestselling *The Unofficial Disney Parks Cookbook*

ADAMS MEDIA

NEW YORK   LONDON   TORONTO   SYDNEY   NEW DELHI

Adams Media
An Imprint of Simon & Schuster, Inc.
100 Technology Center Drive
Stoughton, Massachusetts 02072

First Adams Media hardcover edition June 2022

ADAMS MEDIA and colophon are trademarks of Simon & Schuster.

For information about special discounts for bulk purchases, please contact Simon & Schuster Special Sales at 1-866-506-1949 or business@simonandschuster.com.

The Simon & Schuster Speakers Bureau can bring authors to your live event. For more information or to book an event contact the Simon & Schuster Speakers Bureau at 1-866-248-3049 or visit our website at www.simonspeakers.com.

Interior design by Sylvia McArdle
Interior photographs by Harper Point Photography
Photography chefs: Chase Elder, Christine Tarango
Interior illustrations and maps by Alaya Howard & Priscilla Yuen
Interior images © 123RF

Manufactured in China

10 9 8 7 6 5 4 3 2 1

Library of Congress Cataloging-in-Publication Data
Names: Craft, Ashley, author.
Title: The unofficial Disney parks EPCOT cookbook / Ashley Craft, author of the USA TODAY bestselling The Unofficial Disney Parks Cookbook.
Description: First Adams Media hardcover edition. | Stoughton, Massachusetts: Adams Media, 2022. | Series: Unofficial cookbook | Includes index.
Identifiers: LCCN 2021061083 | ISBN 9781507216804 (hc) | ISBN 9781507216811 (ebook)
Subjects: LCSH: International cooking. | EPCOT Center (Fla.) | BISAC: COOKING / Individual Chefs & Restaurants | TRAVEL / Special Interest / Amusement & Theme Parks | LCGFT: Cookbooks.
Classification: LCC TX725.A1 C638 2022 | DDC 641.59--dc23/eng/20211231
LC record available at https://lccn.loc.gov/2021061083

ISBN 978-1-5072-1680-4
ISBN 978-1-5072-1681-1 (ebook)

Dedication

To my parents, Karen and Jeff Peterson, for giving me cultural experiences on trips around the world and encouraging me to try new foods from different countries. Thank you for supporting me all my life and helping me so much. Love you!

Contents

CHAPTER 4

Entrées **85**

Acknowledgments

As always, this book would not be possible without the support, encouragement, and back rubs given by my husband, Danny. Thank you for not batting an eye at my going to EPCOT three times this year. And thanks to my kids, Elliot, Hazel, and Clifford, for not getting upset at coming on only one of those trips.

Thanks to my parents, Karen and Jeff Peterson, and my in-laws, Tricia and Rick Craft, for your love and excitement for me and my books.

Tricia Craft and Emily Goodsell also keep signing up to read and help me edit my books, and I am insanely grateful that they continue to do so. Thanks for being on my team.

Special thank-you to my little sister, Kelly Merrill, for coming with me to EPCOT and tasting bite after bite after bite of incredible (and filling) festival foods *and* foregoing most of the rides. And thanks to baby Alden for being a sweetie and a stellar travel companion.

Joe Perry, you never stop supporting me and checking in on me and helping me be the best author I can be. You fill me with confidence and make me feel like a rock star.

And to Julia Jacques, Sarah Armour, and Sarah Doughty at Adams Media for answering my myriad emails and for your positive, upbeat attitudes. You worked incredibly hard on every aspect of this book. Thanks for letting me do so many projects at once and for having faith in me to meet my deadlines and provide quality work.

Preface

Walt Disney World Resort currently consists of four major theme parks, two water parks, two entertainment districts, and over twenty-five resort hotels. And that's not even mentioning its myriad waterways, golf courses, trails, restaurants, and other features. Of all these locations, one stands out to me as the most beautiful, the most unique, the most packed with learning *and* flavor: EPCOT. The only park of its kind in the world, EPCOT offers guests an opportunity to see the world as it was, as it is, and as it can be in the future.

When I worked at Walt Disney World Resort in 2010 and 2011, I loved visiting EPCOT to meet and talk with the international employees working in each of the world pavilions. I would ask them where they were from and how they liked living in the US. I would try to learn a simple phrase in their native language. It was a beautiful opportunity to meet people from around the world, in one place, in one afternoon.

During the past year, I traveled to EPCOT three times in order to get the latest look at the festival and country food and drink offerings. My sister Kelly (and her baby Alden) and I hit up every booth and sampled the tasty bites and sips. We got reservations at restaurants and took quick-service snacks to go back to our hotel. And what we decided was not only that EPCOT is an incredible place of global learning and beauty, but also that the food and beverages are out of this world!

I hope you love this book as much as I do. I had so much fun crafting the recipes in my kitchen in Kansas, and my family sure enjoyed tasting exciting cuisines from around the world each night.

Introduction

School Bread, Fish and Chips, Horchata, and Coppa Delizia are just some of the iconic international delights that guests enjoy while touring EPCOT's World Showcase. Of course, you may not have a trip planned to EPCOT in the future. Or maybe you will be visiting soon and want to prep your taste buds for the tantalizing treats you'll soon be trying. Whatever the case, you can now bring the flavors of the world as presented at EPCOT right to your home!

The Unofficial Disney Parks EPCOT Cookbook contains one hundred of the most popular World Showcase and festival foods and drinks served at EPCOT. Here you'll find tasty and easy-to-make dishes you never thought you could make in your own kitchen. This book is organized by course, so you can flip to whatever section fits your occasion. You'll find:

- Appetizers and snacks such as the flavor-filled House-Made Hummus Fries from the Morocco pavilion, smooth and savory Soupe à L'oignon Gratinée (French Onion Soup) from the France pavilion, and beloved School Bread from the Norway pavilion.
- Entrées such as Margherita Pizzas from the Italy pavilion, vegan BBQ Jackfruit Burgers from The American Adventure pavilion, and Gourmet Macaroni and Cheese with Boursin Garlic & Fine Herbs Cheese topped with Herbed Panko from the annual EPCOT International Food & Wine Festival.

- Desserts such as melt-in-your-mouth Pastel de Queso con Cajeta from the Mexico pavilion, bite-sized Banana Cheesecake Egg Rolls from the China pavilion, and gooey Sticky Toffee Pudding from the United Kingdom pavilion.
- Alcoholic and nonalcoholic beverages such as a refreshing Tokyo Sunset from the Japan pavilion, a nostalgic Froot Loops Shake from the EPCOT International Flower & Garden Festival, and an indulgent Sipping Chocolate Flight: White, Milk, and Dark Chocolate from the EPCOT International Festival of the Arts.

There are simple snacks you can whip up at a moment's notice, as well as more intricate meals and treats to wow your family or party guests.

Before putting on your mouse ears and pulling out the mixer, be sure to read through Part 1 for details on the EPCOT countries and festivals you'll explore in the recipes, as well as information about kitchen tools you'll want to have on hand. Even the most seasoned Disney chefs benefit from a little preparation.

Are you ready to begin your culinary trip around the world? It's time to create amazing foods and drinks and, most importantly, magical memories in the kitchen!

EPCOT 101

Welcome to EPCOT! Whether you have been to EPCOT hundreds of times, a few times, or never, there are always mouthwatering dishes and drinks to discover.

In this part, you'll find everything you need to help you whip up the recipes in Part 2. Chapter 1 takes you on a tour of the most iconic and popular foods and drinks served across the eleven countries of World Showcase and EPCOT's three most popular seasonal festivals: EPCOT International Festival of the Arts, EPCOT International Flower & Garden Festival, and EPCOT International Food & Wine Festival. You'll learn just how EPCOT came to be and take a closer look at how the restaurants, beverage carts, and food kiosks are laid out across the park for optimal dining. And before you tie on your favorite Disney apron, check out Chapter 2, which details the equipment you'll want to have on hand to make dishes and drinks worthy of a certain mouse. The delicious magic of EPCOT awaits. Let's dig in!

CHAPTER 1

The EPCOT Experience

The EPCOT World Showcase can come across as overwhelming. There are eleven pavilions, each focused on a different country, as well as countless kiosks and drink carts. So what meals, treats, and sips can you find in the different countries? And exactly how did EPCOT come to be one of Disney's top attractions?

This chapter will answer all of your burning questions and get you excited about enjoying the food and beverages of EPCOT, whether at the park or in the comfort of your own home. You'll first explore a brief history of EPCOT, from its beginnings to the latest news. Then you'll learn more about the tasty offerings and other unique experiences awaiting in each country pavilion and the three main festivals (EPCOT International Festival of the Arts, EPCOT International Flower & Garden Festival, and EPCOT International Food & Wine Festival). Everything you need to know about the magic of EPCOT is here!

The Origins of EPCOT

Walt Disney opened Disneyland in Anaheim, California, in 1955 to wild success. Everyone loved the attractions, food, and family-friendly atmosphere. It seemed like everything he touched turned to gold, as his movies were also soaring across the box office. For Walt, though, it was never enough. One of his key quotes, "Keep moving forward," embodied his unrest and desire for continually achieving greater and bigger things.

In the 1960s, he began looking to his next big project. He didn't want it to be just another theme park: He wanted to do something that would celebrate human achievement and change the world. He unveiled his "Florida Project," which included a section that was something special and unexpected. It was a city—not a pretend city, but an actual city where real people would live, work, and play, with its own homes, public transportation, and sustainable farming. He called that section the Experimental Prototype Community of Tomorrow, or EPCOT. Unfortunately, Walt Disney passed away years before EPCOT was built, and Imagineers didn't feel the same inspiration to create an entire city as Walt did.

In 1982 EPCOT Center (later known just as EPCOT) was finished and opened its doors to the public. Even though it wasn't a community where people lived and worked, The Walt Disney Company did its best to keep to Walt's ideas of celebrating human achievement. The theme park became somewhat of a permanent world's fair, delighting guests from all over with structures, menus, events, and more that showcased the beauty of the world and its diverse cultures.

The Layout of EPCOT

Prior to 2021, EPCOT was divided into two large areas: World Showcase and Future World. World Showcase housed eleven country "pavilions" that represented a diverse subsection of the globe. Future World focused on space exploration, innovations, and technological advancements. Now EPCOT is broken up into four "neighborhoods": World Celebration, World Discovery, World Nature, and World Showcase.

World Celebration includes the iconic Spaceship Earth attraction, lovingly referred to as the "giant golf ball," as well as fountains and shops. World Discovery holds the Mission: Space attraction, the Test Track ride, the Guardians of the Galaxy: Cosmic Rewind ride (scheduled to open summer 2022), and the Space 220 Restaurant. World Nature takes guests on a glider above the earth on the Soarin' simulator, teaches them about gardening on the Living with the Land ride, and brings them along on a deep ocean dive around The Seas with Nemo & Friends pavilion. Lastly, World Showcase remains home to its original eleven country pavilions.

World Showcase

Of the four neighborhoods in EPCOT, World Showcase is where your taste buds take center stage. Guests pour in to experience the delicious adventure of eating and drinking "around the world." When looking at the World Showcase's center lake ahead of you, you'll find the following pavilions from left to right: Mexico, Norway, China, Germany, Italy, The American Adventure, Japan, Morocco, France, United Kingdom, and Canada. There has always been a heated debate on which direction is best to start: Mexico or Canada? But with the opening of Disney Skyliner in 2019, a large portion of guests now enter the park through the International Gateway, which is between the France and UK pavilions—adding more debate about where to start! Wherever you start your own World Showcase journey, you'll get to take in sights, sounds, smells, and tastes from around the world, and hopefully experience things you never have before.

Each pavilion has at least one sit-down restaurant and quick-service restaurant, as well as drink and snack stands and gift shops. Three pavilions also have rides: the Gran Fiesta Tour Starring the Three Caballeros in Mexico, Frozen Ever After (previously Maelstrom) in Norway, and Remy's Ratatouille Adventure in France. Some pavilions have live entertainment, such as the acrobats of China and the chair-balancers of France, and some, such as China and Canada, have Circle-Vision 360 theaters where you can watch a film in 360° and learn more about that country. Every pavilion is detailed and unique and will transport you to amazing locations around the world.

Festivals

In addition to its incredible year-round offerings, EPCOT's World Showcase is also home to several international festivals that transform the park into a marketplace and tasting-ground for specialty merchandise, foods, and drinks. The most popular festivals that happen each year are EPCOT International Festival of the Arts, EPCOT International Flower & Garden Festival, and EPCOT International Food & Wine Festival.

EPCOT International Festival of the Arts
Occurring first in the calendar year, typically through the months of January and February, this festival has been around only since 2017. It highlights visual, culinary, and performing arts. You're likely to see artists doing live demonstrations or chalk drawings, as well as selling their original art

and prints. Collectors will love this event: It's a special opportunity to own unique pieces of art from renowned Disney artists. Food and drink offerings are very colorful and sometimes have an interactive element, like a cookie you can "paint" with frosting yourself!

EPCOT International Flower & Garden Festival

Next up is the EPCOT International Flower & Garden Festival, which usually happens from March through May. In celebration of gardening and sustainable farming, the whole park is decorated with larger-than-life topiaries that seem to appear overnight. Incredible floral displays are around every corner, and you'll even catch your favorite Disney characters looking a bit green as they become garden topiaries. Culinary offerings include more plant-based dishes than other festivals, using vegetables and fruits grown locally at EPCOT and prominently featuring meatless options and meat substitutes. Others just give the impression of gardening, like the Cookie Butter Worms and Dirt drink.

EPCOT International Food & Wine Festival

Arguably the most popular of all the EPCOT festivals, the EPCOT International Food & Wine Festival can run as long as mid-July through late November. All of EPCOT's festivals have incredible food, but this one takes the cake. Food is not a side product of other agendas; it is front and center as the number one reason everyone is there. Celebrity chefs and popular food brands come out to provide demonstrations and tastings to guests. Booths pop up throughout World Showcase, like Shimmering Sips, featuring glittering wines and yummy bites like Plant-Based Banana Bread with Mixed Berry Compote, or the simple moniker "Waffles," selling—you guessed it—incredibly topped waffles! More regions, like Brazil, selling Crispy Pork Belly with Black Beans and Tomato, and Hawaii, with succulent dishes like Teriyaki-Glazed SPAM Hash, are represented in World Showcase. The quantity of new foods and drinks offered during this event is incredible and can take more than one trip to tackle.

Other Festivals

Though not featured in the recipes in this book, EPCOT has another annual festival, the EPCOT International Festival of the Holidays, which is a celebration of different nations' winter holiday traditions. It culminates in the nightly Candlelight Processional where a celebrity guest appears with a choir to tell the story of Christmas. A New Year's Eve festival also occurs each year and additional entertainment comes to EPCOT, including DJs and dance areas around the park. This little festival is wonderful and has fun and delicious foods and drinks to enjoy.

Creating Your Own EPCOT Recipes

EPCOT is a stunning location that has redefined what a theme park can be. A first-of-its-kind showcase of the depth and breadth of human achievement, it stands today as a testament that guests love what it has been offering since 1982. EPCOT is always changing and adapting to new ideas but never straying from its original platform of celebrating the culinary, technological, cultural, and environmental contributions the world has to offer.

In the pages ahead you will find recipes for one hundred of the most iconic and beloved foods and drinks that EPCOT has ever served. Some are no longer available at the park—even more reason to include them here for you to enjoy at home! Check out the following chapter on tools and other kitchen essentials to have on hand before you start cooking. Armed with this equipment and the background information you've just explored about EPCOT, you'll be ready to see the world and taste what it has to offer!

CHAPTER 2

The EPCOT Kitchen Essentials

It's almost time to get cooking! However, before you begin, take a look at this chapter to be sure you have all the equipment you need for successfully making the recipes in this book. People in different countries may work with cookware that you are not used to. A tagine or cannoli tubes might not currently be in your pantry, but having them on hand will allow you to take a culinary trip to Morocco or Italy whenever the mood strikes!

While this list may seem intimidating at first, there are substitutions you can make for supplies you may not have. The tools and staples are also ordered alphabetically, so you can flip back to a specific section at any time. Soon you'll be whipping up magical recipes sure to get stamps in your foodie passport.

Equipment and Food Staples

The world within EPCOT awaits you, but are you ready to get cooking? Before you start, take a look through this section to make sure your kitchen is stocked with all the tools to make the recipes in Part 2.

Baking Sheets

Baking sheets come in many shapes and sizes, but the best ones for the recipes in this book have $\frac{1}{2}$"-tall sides and are called "half sheets."

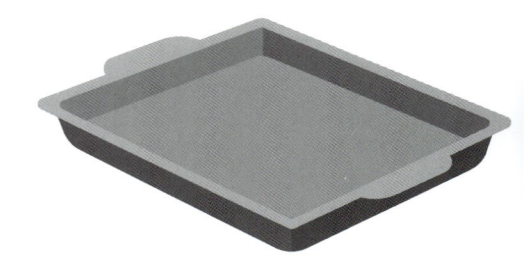

Blender

A good-quality, high-powered stand blender will help you achieve a smoother consistency for smoothies and dips than a less expensive option, but both will get the job done. Start with a low setting and turn up the speed as larger ingredient pieces break up.

Cake Pans

Standard 9" circle and square cake pans will help you create cakes and other delicious dishes. Typically, you line these pans with parchment paper to prevent sticking.

Cannoli Tubes

If you don't own cannoli tubes yet, look for them online. They are thin silver metal tubes that are used to wrap cannoli dough around while the shells are frying. Cannoli cannot be made without these tubes since they have to be submerged in extremely hot oil. Do not attempt to make your own cannoli tubes!

Cocktail Shaker

Many of the drink recipes in this book call for the use of a cocktail shaker. This makes mixing easy for single-serve drinks, especially if a thicker syrup is used. You can quickly chill a drink during mixing by adding ice to the shaker before shaking. If you don't have a cocktail shaker, whisk the mixture well without ice in a large glass or small bowl and strain through a sieve into the drinking glass/cup of choice.

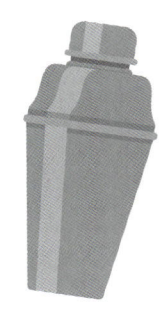

Coffee Substitute

Some people are not partial to coffee, or might want to enjoy a coffee-style beverage later in the day without the surge of caffeine it usually comes with. Many coffee-substitute products are available at stores and online retailers that provide a natural caffeine- and coffee-free experience. Most are made from malted barley, chicory, and rye. Pero and Caf-Lib are great choices, as they don't require a coffee machine to brew. Simply follow the instructions on the packaging, then add to the recipe in place of coffee.

Cooling Rack

A common wire cooling/drying rack is sufficient for the recipes in this book. They are typically made from stainless steel and have straight lines or a crosshatch pattern.

Electric Pressure Cooker

Electric pressure cookers can save a lot of time in the kitchen and provide a delicious product. Many different brands are available. Make sure that there is a properly sized inner pot placed in the cooker and that you are careful to avoid steam burns when you release the pressure.

Food Coloring

Many of the following recipes use food coloring to pull off the original Disney look. Gel colors are always preferred for solid foods and liquid colors for drinks. Gel colors have a brighter pop of color than liquid food coloring, and the tighter consistency won't change the texture of the dish. If your gel colors come in pots and cannot "drop," use a wooden toothpick to dip into the gel and swipe it through the food you want to color. Repeat for each drop needed.

Food Processor

Food processors are high-powered blenders that specialize in chopping dry foods. If you don't have a food processor, a blender works almost as well. If you have neither, chopping very finely with a knife works too.

Glass Pan

A glass pan is needed to make Mocha Tiramisù. The standard size is 8" × 8" and works best for this recipe. A metal pan can be substituted. Just be sure to check the food more often if using a metal pan to prevent overcooking.

Grill or Grill Pan

For items that need to be grilled, an outdoor grill and indoor grill pan are interchangeable for searing. Propane grills should be preheated to ensure even cooking. Indoor grill pans need to be greased with cooking oil before using to help prevent sticking. Charcoal grills can also be used; they just require more prep and cleanup. Consult your grill instructions for safe cooking guidelines. Smoked meats will need to be smoked using a smoker or a gas grill with a smoker box. Consult the recipes and the Smoker Box section for more information.

Ice Cream Machine

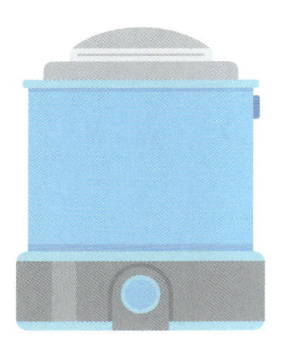

The easiest ice cream machines to use are the ones with a freezable "bowl." This bowl is removed from the freezer moments before use, and cream or drink mix is poured directly into the frozen bowl. The bowl then spins on a base, and a paddle mixes and scrapes the inside. Other options are available if you are unable to use this type of ice cream machine. For example, you can use an ice cream bucket-type machine that requires ice cubes and rock salt. Just pour the mixture from the recipe into the metal inner container and fill the outer bucket with ice and rock salt. Run the machine until the consistency matches the recipe description.

Immersion Blender

Immersion blenders are convenient because you can leave your soup or sauce in the pot and purée it without moving the mixture to a stand blender or food processor. If you don't have one, a blender or food processor works just as well.

Kitchen Torch

A kitchen torch is needed for the Key Lime Tarts and Maple Crème Brûlée recipes. Torches are generally available at big-box stores and online, but if you'd rather not get one, place tarts on a baking sheet and place close to the heating element in an oven and watch carefully while broiling on high. You can also omit toasting.

Long Silicone Mold

A long silicone mold is needed for the Passion Fruit Mousse with Dragon Fruit Jam, Key Lime Tarts, and Strawberry Mousse with Chocolate Crisp Pearls recipes in this book. If you don't have one, you can purchase one from an online retailer. The mold these recipes were created with was 3" long by 1" wide and 1" deep. The dimensions don't need to be precise; the mold just needs to be long and deep enough to hold the ingredients.

Mini Bundt Pan

A mini Bundt pan is used in the Sticky Toffee Pudding recipe. The shape allows for even cooking and a well for the sauce to be poured. Ones made of silicone are best because they can be twisted and pushed to release the cake. If you don't have a mini Bundt pan, you can purchase one online. If you don't want to buy one, a standard muffin tin will work. Just flip the tin upside down when cooled to release the pudding.

Muffin Tins

The only type of muffin tin you will need for this book is a jumbo-sized muffin tin. These typically have six large cups instead of the standard twelve smaller cups. Generously grease the tin with cooking oil first to prevent sticking.

Paper Grocery Bags

The Maple Popcorn recipe in this book uses a large paper grocery bag to mix the toppings with the popcorn. This method ensures an even coating and flavor distribution. If you do not have access to a large (clean and unused) paper grocery bag, you can simply toss the seasonings and popcorn together in an extra-large bowl.

Parchment Paper

Almost every recipe in this book that requires baking will instruct you to line your baking sheet or pan with parchment paper. This simple step ensures a more even baking surface and more consistent browning, and greatly reduces the likelihood of your food sticking to the sheet or pan. Parchment paper can be found in any grocery store.

Pie Pan

A pie pan is needed for Pastel de Queso con Cajeta. A glass or aluminum pan will work well. Be sure to grease the pan generously with cooking oil or spray to avoid sticking.

Piping Bags

Many recipes in this book call for piping bags, but you don't have to own a fancy set. A heavy-duty plastic sandwich or gallon bag will do. Simply load the dough or other mixture into the bag, then snip a small edge off one of the bottom corners. Start your hole out small and make it bigger as needed. (Some recipes will call for special piping bag tips. While you don't need to use a tip for any recipe that follows, it can make for an eye-catching design.)

Pots and Pans

Heavy-bottomed pots and saucepans are preferred in the recipes in this book. The thick metal bottom regulates the temperature better and prevents burning. If you don't have heavy-bottomed pots and pans, any appropriately sized pot or pan will do; just keep an extra-close eye on foods cooking on the stove. Stir more frequently to prevent burning.

Ramekins

Ramekin is just a fancy word for a small glass or ceramic bowl that can be baked in the oven. Recipes like Queso Fundido and Maple Crème Brûlée call for these bowls. If you don't have designated ramekins, check the bottom of your glass storage containers or cereal bowls to see if they are oven-proof. The Queso Fundido recipe calls for a wider ramekin, about 4"–5" in diameter, while the Maple Crème Brûlée can be made in a smaller ramekin, about 3"–4" in diameter.

Rolling Pin

Rolling pins come in many shapes and sizes, including those that have handles on the sides, French styles, and the straight cylindrical stye. Any variety is fine for use in the following recipes. To get an even flatter and more even press, consider a pasta roller for the Cannoli recipe.

Shaved Ice Machine

The Tangerine Kakigōri recipe calls for a shaved ice machine. These range from multi-thousand-dollar machines that expertly shave the ice using a razor-thin blade to more affordable models found in most grocery or big-box stores. Any machine you have is fine. It is difficult to shave ice without a specialized machine; however, some high-end blenders have the capability to crush ice finely enough to use in this recipe.

Sieve/Sifter

The sifters and sieves described in the following recipes refer to a stainless-steel mesh half-dome strainer. Get one with a medium-fine mesh.

Smoker Box

A smoker box is a handy tool that essentially turns your propane or charcoal grill into a smoker. It is a small metal box with holes in the top and can be purchased at online retailers. Set up your grill by placing the smoker box as close to one heating element as possible, on one side of the grill. Fill the box with soaked wood chips (see Wood Chips section in this chapter) and ignite the heating element under the box to the lowest heat setting. Your meat should be placed as far from the smoker box as possible, on the other side of the grill, with the other heating elements off. This will create a cycle of smoke that rises over the box and fills the grill with smoke. This will infuse your meat with smoke flavor and cook it slowly and tenderly. Follow smoker box packaging instructions for more details.

Stand Mixer

Almost any recipe in this book that requires mixing uses a stand mixer. This machine makes mixing, whipping, and kneading easy and uniform. If you don't have a stand mixer, the next best option is a hand mixer. These often also have interchangeable attachments for mixing or whipping. If you have neither, you can certainly mix, whip, and knead by hand—it will just take a bit more strength and stamina.

Sushi Mat

In the recipe for California Rolls, the use of a sushi mat is optional; however, a sushi mat will help you roll and squeeze the sushi roll simultaneously to ensure your roll does not pop open. If you don't have a sushi mat, use a sheet of strong parchment paper.

Syrups

Syrups are a key part of making many mixed drinks. Walt Disney World Resort typically uses the brand Monin for its drinks instead of house-made syrups. This provides consistency and high quality across the resort and is especially useful when drinks change locations—which they often do. If you can't find Monin syrups, other brands work just as well.

Tagine

A tagine is a specialized cooking dish from Morocco that features a conical lid made of clay. The shape traps rising steam and returns the moisture back down to the food, creating flavorful and moist meals. While tagines can be easily acquired online, they can be pricey. If you don't have one, feel free to use a Dutch oven or other sturdy heatproof pot with a lid.

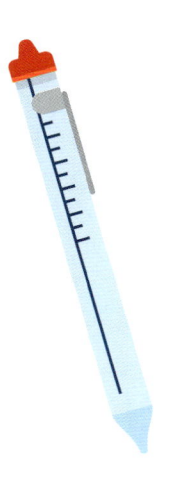

Thermometers

A confection or candy thermometer is essential for any candy making or deep-frying. Bringing mixtures to the correct temperature changes the final product's texture and taste. A meat thermometer is crucial to ensure that meat is cooked to a safe temperature. Both types of thermometers can be bought at most grocery and big-box stores, as well as online.

Wood Chips

Wood chips used in smoking meats are sold in bags at grocery and big-box stores and come in many varieties. It's recommended that you use hickory for the relevant recipes in this book, but other wood chips will work and will provide unique flavor profiles. Soak wood chips in a large bowl of water at least 30 minutes before you plan to smoke your meats. Keep chips submerged while grilling, then strain individual handfuls before placing them into the smoker box.

Getting Started

Now that you've explored the tools, ingredients, and other special items used in the recipes in this book, you're ready to mix, blend, freeze, cook, shake, and more! Remember: The dishes ahead are your wonderful artwork! Although each recipe was modeled after an EPCOT original, your creations are unique to you. Experiment with flavors, colors, and presentation as you please. It's time to make some delicious magic!

PART 2

Delicious Dishes

Now that you have a deeper understanding of EPCOT and the equipment to add to your kitchen staples, you're ready to get cooking! The following chapters hold the secrets to the amazing flavors of EPCOT's meals, snacks, cocktails, and more. There are one hundred recipes that are served in the eleven countries of World Showcase and the three major festivals of EPCOT. Instead of covering the mile-long World Showcase circle, you only need to flip the page to discover fan favorites, as well as soon-to-be go-tos!

The chapters in this part are organized by type to make things even easier. Cook, eat, and sip your way through appetizers and snacks, entrées, desserts, and drinks, or skip around to the recipes that stand out to you. However you travel through these recipes, do so with an open mind and stomach: Some of the ingredients or foods may be new to you, but don't let that stop you from trying them out! One may just become your next dinner or party staple.

CHAPTER 3

Appetizers and Snacks

The appetizers and snacks of EPCOT are smaller bites from around the globe. Instead of a hot dog, how about Bratwursts piled high with sauerkraut from Germany? And instead of the same old French fries, how about House-Made Hummus Fries, teeming with spices from Morocco? Who wants canned tomato soup when you can easily make a fresh batch like the kind served during the EPCOT International Festival of the Arts? Your friends will be so impressed when you show up to the party with a Watermelon Salad draped in homemade pickled onions, instead of the standard watermelon slices.

Wherever you serve or take the dishes in this chapter, let them take you to a whole new world of flavors and experiences!

Queso Fundido

San Angel Inn Restaurante, Mexico Pavilion

Unlike the queso that many Americans are familiar with—a creamy cheese blend eaten with tortilla chips—this melty cheese begins to solidify again in a matter of minutes, so have your appetite ready! Instead of dipping chips, use a spoon to scoop a generous helping of cheese, chorizo, peppers, and onions onto a flour tortilla. Roll it up and take a big bite.

SERVES 2

½ cup ground chorizo

¼ medium yellow onion, peeled and sliced into strips

½ medium poblano pepper, sliced into strips

6 ounces shredded Monterey jack cheese

4 (6") flour tortillas

1. Preheat broiler to high with rack in top of oven.
2. In a small skillet over medium-high heat, brown chorizo until cooked through, 5–8 minutes. Drain and set chorizo aside.
3. In same skillet over medium-high heat, cook onion and pepper 5–10 minutes until soft. Set aside.
4. Place cheese in an ungreased 6" ramekin. Place chorizo, onion, and pepper in the middle of cheese. Place dish on top rack of oven and broil 2–3 minutes until cheese is melted and bubbly but not burnt.
5. Immediately scoop cheese mixture into tortillas, roll up, and serve.

Guacamole

La Hacienda de San Angel, Mexico Pavilion

You've likely eaten guacamole plenty of times and even made it at home. However, this version stands out from the rest due to the mango and pepitas. The sweet and juicy mango gives a stark contrast to the creaminess of the avocado, and the pepitas add a satisfying crunch! La Hacienda de San Angel serves its Guacamole with chicharrones drizzled in Salsa Valentina (a bottled hot sauce from Mexico), but if that's not your style, tortilla chips work great too.

SERVES 2

- 1 large ripe avocado, peeled and pitted
- 1 tablespoon restaurant-style mild salsa
- 1/8 teaspoon garlic powder
- 1 tablespoon lime juice
- 2 tablespoons diced fresh mango
- 2 tablespoons crushed pepitas
- 2 cups chicharrones
- 1 tablespoon Salsa Valentina

In a small bowl, mash avocado with a fork. Add salsa, garlic powder, and lime juice. Stir until well combined. Top with mango and pepitas. Lay out chicharrones on a medium plate and drizzle with Salsa Valentina. Serve immediately alongside Guacamole.

EPCOT Park Tip

The right time to eat at La Hacienda de San Angel is during a fireworks show at EPCOT. A window seat will give you a wonderful view of the lake and all the entertainment going on out there. Even if you can't get a reservation during a show, the food is reason enough to snag a seat.

School Bread

Kringla Bakeri Og Kafe, Norway Pavilion

This recipe has become quite the fan favorite. However, people from the world outside the US have asked: What is instant vanilla pudding? As it turns out, this is an American staple that can be difficult to find in other countries. If you can't get instant vanilla pudding in your area, simply swap for an equal amount of vanilla custard!

SERVES 8

3 tablespoons salted butter, melted

2 cups warm water (110°F)

5 cups all-purpose flour

4 tablespoons granulated sugar

1/2 teaspoon ground cinnamon

4 tablespoons active dry yeast

1 cup confectioners' sugar

3 tablespoons heavy cream

1 teaspoon vanilla extract

1 (3.4-ounce) box instant vanilla pudding

1 1/2 cups whole milk

1 cup sweetened shredded coconut

1. Grease a large bowl with nonstick cooking spray. Set aside.
2. In the bowl of a stand mixer, add butter, warm water, flour, granulated sugar, cinnamon, and yeast. Using the dough hook attachment, knead 5 minutes. Then place in greased bowl. Cover with plastic wrap and let rise in a warm place 30 minutes.
3. Preheat oven to 375°F. Line an ungreased baking sheet with parchment paper and set aside.
4. Turn dough out onto lightly floured surface and cut into eight equal pieces. Form each piece into a ball by tucking excess dough under and creating a taut top. Place on prepared baking sheet, evenly spaced apart, and allow to rise an additional 5 minutes.
5. Bake dough 12 minutes, until golden brown. Let cool on baking sheet 10 minutes.

(continued on next page)

6. In a small shallow bowl, stir together confectioners' sugar and cream. Set aside. In a separate medium bowl, whisk together vanilla, instant vanilla pudding, and milk. Chill pudding mixture 5 minutes, then spoon into a piping bag fitted with any size tip. Pour coconut into another shallow bowl and set aside.

7. To assemble: Cut a 1" hole out of the top of each bun. Pull out or push down bread inside bun. Invert bun and dip whole top side into the cream mixture. Then immediately roll in coconut. Pipe pudding into the hole and fill inside of bun, ending with a small swirl on top of bun.

Did You Know?

Did you know the attraction in the Norway pavilion before Frozen Ever After *was called* Maelstrom? *Meaning "powerful whirlpool," this ride delivered with nasty trolls that sent guests flowing backward along a winding river. Now guests of* Frozen Ever After *can experience the same motion—but instead of nasty trolls, it's Elsa that blows them backward!*

California Rolls

Kabuki Cafe, Japan Pavilion

It's interesting that California Rolls are served in the Japan pavilion at EPCOT, because, as the name suggests, they originated in Los Angeles. A Japanese chef in the 1960s was trying to market sushi to hesitant Americans and decided to replace pricey tuna with readily available avocados and "hide" the seaweed paper with rice to make the dish seem less foreign. It certainly worked; California rolls are now one of the most popular sushi dishes in the world.

SERVES 2

- 1½ cups short-grain rice, cooked
- 4 tablespoons plus 2 teaspoons rice vinegar, divided
- 3 tablespoons plus 1 teaspoon granulated sugar, divided
- 1 teaspoon salt
- ¼ cup mayonnaise
- 2 full sheets nori seaweed
- ½ medium cucumber, sliced into long, thin pieces
- 1 medium avocado, peeled, pitted, and sliced
- 2 tablespoons smelt roe
- 4 sticks imitation crab
- 2 tablespoons soy sauce
- 2 tablespoons pickled ginger
- 2 teaspoons wasabi

1. Pour cooked rice into a large (preferably wooden) bowl and stir 3 minutes to release heat. Add 4 tablespoons rice vinegar, 3 tablespoons sugar, and salt and stir to combine. Set aside.

2. Make Japanese mayonnaise by combining mayonnaise, remaining 2 teaspoons rice vinegar, and remaining 1 teaspoon sugar in a small bowl. Set aside.

3. Lay nori sheets on plastic wrap–covered sushi mat. Wet your hands and scoop about ½ cup rice mixture into your hands. Cover each nori sheet in a thin layer of rice. Flip each sheet over on plastic wrap. Spread 1–2 tablespoons Japanese mayonnaise down the middle of long side of each sheet. Place equal amounts cucumber, avocado, smelt roe, and imitation crab on top of mayonnaise.

4. Carefully roll into tight tubes. Wet a sharp knife and slice each roll into bite-sized pieces. Repeat with remaining nori and fillings.

5. Serve with soy sauce, pickled ginger, and wasabi on the side.

House-Made
Crab and Cheese Wontons

Lotus House, China Pavilion

This recipe calls for imitation crab, which offers the taste and texture of crab without the big price tag. However, if you want to splurge, try real crab! If crab isn't your thing, an equal amount of shrimp, lobster, or crayfish can be swapped in. For a vegan version, replace the crab with an equal amount of peas, carrots, or jackfruit, and leave out the Worcestershire sauce.

YIELDS 20 WONTONS

48 ounces vegetable oil, for frying
3/4 cup shredded imitation crab
4 ounces cream cheese, softened
2 medium green onions, sliced thin
1/4 teaspoon garlic powder
1 teaspoon Worcestershire sauce
20 wonton wrappers
1/4 cup water

1. Heat oil in a large pot over medium heat to 350°F. Line a large plate with paper towels.
2. In a small bowl, mix together crab, cream cheese, green onions, garlic powder, and Worcestershire sauce.
3. Lay out 1 wonton wrapper at a time and place 1 teaspoon filling in center of wrapper. Dip finger in water and dab center of each long edge of wrapper with wet finger. Bring opposite edges of wrapper together and pinch closed along edges.
4. Carefully lower 3–4 wontons at a time into hot oil and fry 1–3 minutes or until golden brown and crispy. Transfer to prepared plate and repeat with remaining wontons. Serve immediately.

Cooking Technique

Getting out a big pot of oil and heating it up to temperature can be a hassle. If you have an air fryer, a similar taste and texture can be achieved with much less effort. Just spray your wontons with nonstick cooking spray and air fry at 325°F for 10 minutes.

Pork Egg Rolls

Lotus Blossom Café, China Pavilion

These egg rolls are divine deep-fried, but a less messy (and slightly healthier) option is to air fry them! Preheat your air fryer to 325°F. Place prepared egg rolls in fry tray and spray with a bit of cooking oil. Cook 10 minutes, flipping them over halfway through the cook time. The result is egg rolls with more of a "baked" taste. Both ways are delicious and easy.

YIELDS 12 EGG ROLLS

1 pound ground pork
1 teaspoon minced fresh ginger
1 teaspoon garlic powder
1 teaspoon salt
1/2 teaspoon ground black pepper
48 ounces vegetable oil, for frying
1 (8-ounce) bag tri-color coleslaw
1 large egg, beaten
12 egg roll wrappers

1. In a medium skillet over medium-high heat, brown ground pork 5–10 minutes until cooked through to 160°F. Add ginger, garlic powder, salt, and pepper. Stir to combine Remove from heat and drain.

2. Heat oil in a medium pot over medium heat to 375°F. Line a large plate with paper towels.

3. Mix coleslaw into pork.

4. Lay out 1 egg roll wrapper at a time with one corner pointing toward you. Brush a bit of beaten egg all the way down opposite two sides. Scoop 2–3 tablespoons pork mixture in center of wrapper. Fold corner closest to you over filling, fold in sides, and finish by rolling onto egg-brushed sides. Set aside and repeat with remaining wrappers and filling.

5. Carefully lower 3–4 egg rolls into hot oil. Cook 1–3 minutes until wrappers are golden brown and bubbly. Transfer to prepared plate and repeat with remaining egg rolls. Serve immediately.

Bratwursts

Sommerfest, Germany Pavilion

Many people have heard about the German celebration of Oktoberfest—but have you heard of Sommerfest? It is an annual festival held in Stuttgart each August. The festival boasts half a million visitors every year. Delicious bites are served while guests dance in the open air to music from around the world. Sommerfest at EPCOT is named after this fabulous fest and offers the taste of summer to hungry parkgoers.

SERVES 6

For Sauerkraut

1/2 large head green cabbage, sliced thin
3/4 cup water
1/4 cup white distilled vinegar
1 tablespoon salt
1/2 teaspoon garlic powder
1/4 teaspoon onion powder
1/4 teaspoon ground black pepper

For Bratwursts

6 (4-ounce) bratwurst sausages
6 bratwurst rolls

1. To make Sauerkraut: In a large saucepan over medium heat, add all Sauerkraut ingredients. Cover and stir occasionally 25–30 minutes until mixture is wilted and reduced in size. Pour into a large Mason jar, cover, and refrigerate 2 hours.
2. To make Bratwursts: Preheat grill on medium-high.
3. Grill sausages until cooked through and internal temperature reaches 160°F, 5–10 minutes. Place into rolls and top with generous helpings of sauerkraut. Serve immediately.

Simplification Hack

American grocery stores don't have as much variety as German ones when it comes to sauerkraut selection, but almost any grocery store carries some options if you're looking to save some time in the kitchen.

Jumbo Pretzels

Sommerfest, Germany Pavilion

Pretzels are a classic American snack, but they actually originated in Germany. A large soft pretzel with a deep brown exterior pairs perfectly with a pint of German beer. At EPCOT, Jumbo Pretzels come in the iconic twisted and pressed pretzel shape, but yours can be in any shape you can imagine. Let the kids get creative!

SERVES 2

2½ cups warm water (110°F), divided
1½ tablespoons dark molasses
1 (0.25-ounce) package active dry yeast
3 tablespoons salted butter, softened
4 cups all-purpose flour
½ teaspoon salt
2 tablespoons baking soda
2 tablespoons coarse salt
2 tablespoons salted butter, melted

1. Combine 1½ cups warm water, molasses, and yeast in a small bowl and let bloom 10 minutes until froth forms on top.

2. In the bowl of a stand mixer fitted with a dough hook attachment, cream softened butter, flour, and salt. Add yeast mixture. Knead mixture in bowl or by hand 8 minutes or until dough is soft and elastic.

3. Cut dough in half and work with one half at a time. Slowly and carefully roll and pull dough into a 4'-long rope. Create a *U* shape by holding up each end, then cross the ends and bring them back down toward the bottom of the *U*. Pull ends back toward sides of pretzel and pinch ends onto pretzel. Repeat with second dough piece. Place each pretzel on a piece of parchment paper and trim paper close to dough. Allow dough to rest 20 minutes.

(continued on next page)

4. Place a baking sheet upside down on middle rack in oven and preheat to 500°F.
5. Pour remaining 1 cup warm water and baking soda into a small saucepan over medium-high heat and bring to a boil. Remove from heat. Brush generously onto each pretzel and sprinkle with coarse salt.
6. Carefully slide 1 pretzel with parchment paper onto preheated pan in oven. Bake at 500°F 10–15 minutes until deep brown. Remove from oven and repeat with remaining pretzel. Brush finished pretzels with melted butter as they come out of the oven and serve immediately.

Mix It Up!

Pretzels can be great vehicles for amazing flavors! Instead of the EPCOT-served salt, try topping with cinnamon sugar, a garlic and herb butter, or some spicy tajin seasoning. Any way you make your pretzels will be fabulous.

Parfait aux Fruits

Les Halles Boulangerie-Patisserie, France Pavilion

Homemade yogurt is incredibly easy to make and can take the guesswork out of breakfast. If you have an electric pressure cooker, you just add the ingredients, press a button, and walk away. And the toppings are endlessly interchangeable. Feel free to replace the homemade raspberry syrup topping in this recipe with homemade or store-bought jams of any flavor. Use any fruits, nuts, or granola for topping. How does blackberry yogurt with mango slices sound? The possibilities are waiting for you to discover them!

SERVES 8

For Yogurt

52 ounces ultra-
   pasteurized whole
   milk, divided
1/2 cup sweetened
   condensed milk
1 cup heavy cream
1 teaspoon vanilla
   extract

For Raspberry Topping

1 cup fresh or frozen
   raspberries
1 cup granulated sugar
1 tablespoon lemon juice

1. To make Yogurt: Pour 1 cup whole milk into a medium microwave-safe bowl and heat in microwave on high 1 minute. Stir and microwave 1 minute more. Add sweetened condensed milk and stir until dissolved.

2. Pour mixture into inner pot of an electric pressure cooker. Add remaining whole milk, cream, and vanilla. Stir well. Close electric pressure cooker lid but leave venting valve open. Press Yogurt button and set to 8 hours.

3. When the 8 hours is complete, remove inner electric pressure cooker pot, cover with plastic wrap, and refrigerate 4 hours up to overnight. Once Yogurt is completely chilled, stir well and place in sealable plastic containers. Leftover Yogurt can be kept in sealed individual containers or one large container in refrigerator up to 1 week.

(continued on next page)

For Assembly

**8 medium fresh
strawberries, hulled
32 fresh blueberries
24 fresh raspberries**

4. To make Raspberry Topping: Combine raspberries, sugar, and lemon juice in a small saucepan over medium heat. Stir and mash raspberries until mixture comes to a boil, then remove from heat. Pour through a sieve into a small container and refrigerate until completely chilled, at least 2 hours up to overnight. Leftover Raspberry Topping can be stored in a sealed plastic container in refrigerator up to 1 week.

5. To assemble: Scoop 2 tablespoons Yogurt into each of eight small clear cups. Layer with 1 tablespoon Raspberry Topping, then $1/4$ cup Yogurt. Top with strawberries and blueberries. Drop a bit of syrup into each fresh raspberry and place 3 raspberries on top of each cup. Serve.

Crunchy Arancini

Via Napoli Ristorante e Pizzeria, Italy Pavilion

If you happen to be in Southern Italy on December 13, you may see people eating arancini. This is the feast day of Santa Lucia, where breads and pastas are ceremoniously not eaten to remember the harsh famine that ended on December 13, 1646, when a grain shipment arrived. Of course, you don't have to wait until December to eat this delicious appetizer. Crunchy Arancini makes a scrumptious finger food fit for any occasion.

YIELDS 8 ARANCINI

2 cups prepared instant risotto

1/2 cup finely grated Pecorino Romano cheese

1/2 cup finely grated mozzarella cheese

1 cup finely grated Parmesan cheese, divided

1/2 cup cooked lean ground beef

1 1/2 cups marinara sauce, divided

3 large eggs, divided

1 teaspoon salt

1/2 teaspoon ground black pepper

1 cup Italian-style bread crumbs

48 ounces vegetable oil, for frying

3 teaspoons chopped fresh parsley

1. In a large bowl, use your hands to mix together risotto, Pecorino Romano, mozzarella, 1/2 cup Parmesan, ground beef, 1/2 cup marinara sauce, 1 egg, salt, and pepper. Divide mixture into eight pieces and squish with your hands to form balls, each about the size of a tangerine.

2. In a small bowl, beat remaining 2 eggs. In another small bowl, pour bread crumbs. Dip and roll each ball in egg, then coat in bread crumbs. Place balls on a large plate and refrigerate to set, about 20 minutes.

3. Heat oil in a large pot over medium-high heat to 350°F. Line a large plate with paper towels.

4. Gently place 2–3 arancini at a time in hot oil and fry 2–5 minutes until bread crumbs are golden brown. Transfer to prepared plate and repeat with remaining arancini.

5. To serve, spoon remaining marinara sauce on small plates and place 2–3 arancini in sauce. Sprinkle with remaining 1/2 cup Parmesan and parsley.

Power Greens Salad

Regal Eagle Smokehouse, The American Adventure Pavilion

This quick-service restaurant is known for its tender smoked meats served in various styles from across the United States. Sometimes, to break up a meaty meal, a nice refreshing salad is in order. This one certainly fits the bill, with a tangy dressing and an array of lettuce with fun toppings. The citrus adds a pop of bright flavor designed to balance out the heavy meats.

SERVES 4

3/4 cup olive oil
1/4 cup apple cider vinegar
3 tablespoons lemon juice
3 tablespoons pulp-free orange juice
4 tablespoons granulated sugar
Zest of 1/2 medium lemon
1 teaspoon salt
1/2 teaspoon ground black pepper
8 cups mixed salad greens
4 tablespoons roasted, salted sunflower seeds
4 tablespoons dried cranberries
1 medium orange, peeled and diced
2 medium radishes, sliced thin

1. In a small bowl or 8-ounce Mason jar, add olive oil, apple cider vinegar, lemon and orange juices, sugar, lemon zest, salt, and pepper. Mix or shake well until combined. Dressing will last in a sealed jar up to 1 week in refrigerator.

2. For each serving, place 2 cups mixed salad greens in a large bowl and top with 1 tablespoon sunflower seeds, 1 tablespoon cranberries, 1 quarter diced orange, and 1/2 sliced radish. Drizzle with citrus dressing and toss to combine.

Menchi Katsu Sliders

Katsura Grill, Japan Pavilion

It's hard to believe, but meat was not eaten in Japan until the mid-1800s. Before then, inhabitants ate a diet of plants and fish. Western cultures entered the country in the 1800s and brought with them meat, which the Japanese then began to incorporate into their meals. *Menchi* means "minced," since this dish is made of minced meat instead of a solid cutlet. The flavors of the beef and bread crumbs nicely offset the acidity of the slaw. Serve alongside French fries.

SERVES 6

48 ounces vegetable oil, for frying
1/2 pound lean ground beef
1 cup panko bread crumbs
1 1/2 teaspoons salt, divided
3/4 teaspoon ground black pepper, divided
1 tablespoon rice vinegar
1 teaspoon pure honey
1 teaspoon minced fresh ginger
1 teaspoon minced fresh garlic
1 teaspoon sesame oil
1 teaspoon soy sauce
2 cups tri-color coleslaw
6 slider buns
6 tablespoons mayonnaise

1. Heat oil in a large pot over medium-high heat to 360°F. Line a large plate with paper towels.
2. Divide ground beef into six equal parts, then shape into patties about 2"–3" in diameter.
3. Pour panko into a small shallow dish and add 1 teaspoon salt and 1/2 teaspoon pepper. Stir well. Cover each patty in panko until well coated.
4. Carefully place 2–3 patties in hot oil and fry 2–5 minutes until patties are golden brown and reach an internal temperature of 160°F. Transfer to prepared plate and repeat with remaining patties.
5. In a medium bowl, stir together rice vinegar, honey, ginger, garlic, sesame oil, soy sauce, remaining 1/2 teaspoon salt, and remaining 1/4 teaspoon pepper. Add coleslaw and mix to combine.
6. Assemble sliders by topping each bottom bun with 1/3 cup coleslaw mixture, 1 patty, 1 tablespoon mayonnaise, and top bun. Insert a skewer through top of each slider. Serve immediately.

Melomakarona

Oasis Sweets & Sips, Morocco Pavilion

Although you may not have eaten (or even heard of) these cookies before, the flavors might taste familiar. They are very festive! The spices mixed with the orange juice are distinctly yuletide—and for a good reason. In Greece, Melomakarona are traditional Christmas cookies served alongside other holiday favorites.

YIELDS 12 COOKIES

For Cookies

1 cup salted butter, softened
3/4 cup granulated sugar
3 large egg yolks
4 cups all-purpose flour
2 teaspoons ground cinnamon
1 teaspoon ground cloves
1/2 teaspoon ground nutmeg
2 teaspoons baking powder
1 teaspoon baking soda
1/2 cup pulp-free orange juice
1 tablespoon pure honey

For Topping

1/2 cup water
1/2 cup pure honey
1/2 cup granulated sugar
2 tablespoons white sesame seeds

1. To make Cookies: Preheat oven to 350°F. Line a baking sheet with parchment paper.
2. In the bowl of a stand mixer, cream butter, sugar, and egg yolks 1 minute. Add flour, cinnamon, cloves, nutmeg, baking powder, and baking soda. Mix 1 minute. Add orange juice and honey. Mix until well combined and a dough forms.
3. Use a 2-tablespoon cookie scoop to portion dough out into balls, then use your hands to shape balls into ovals. Place ovals on prepared baking sheet and bake 15–20 minutes until bottoms are slightly browned.
4. To make Topping: Combine water, honey, and sugar in a small saucepan over medium heat. Bring to a boil, then remove from heat. When Cookies are done, generously brush with Topping and sprinkle with sesame seeds while still hot. Serve immediately.

House-Made Hummus Fries

Spice Road Table, Morocco Pavilion

Calling these "fries" is a stretch; they are more like hummus "bars." But no matter what you want to call them, you are going to be blown away by the incredible flavor packed into each bite. If they get crumbly, don't fret. Just grab a fork!

YIELDS 10 FRIES

2 (14.5-ounce) cans garbanzo beans, drained and rinsed
2 tablespoons ground cumin
1 teaspoon ancho chili powder
1 tablespoon ground coriander
1 tablespoon paprika
2 tablespoons dried cilantro
2 tablespoons minced fresh garlic
1 tablespoon salt
1 tablespoon lemon juice
¼ cup garbanzo bean flour
48 ounces vegetable oil, for frying

1. Blend garbanzo beans in a food processor or blender until a paste is formed.
2. Scoop paste into a medium bowl and add cumin, ancho chili powder, coriander, paprika, cilantro, garlic, salt, lemon juice, and garbanzo bean flour. Stir until well combined.
3. Line an 8" × 8" glass or metal pan with parchment paper and scoop mixture into pan. Firmly press mixture into pan with spatula and freeze 1 hour. Remove pan from freezer and cut into bars approximately 1" × 3". Freeze 4 more hours.
4. Heat oil in a large pan over medium heat to 325°F. Carefully remove each hummus bar from pan and gently slide 2–3 bars at a time into hot oil. Fry 1–4 minutes until golden brown. Transfer to prepared plate and repeat with remaining bars. Serve immediately.

Mix It Up!

Play around with the spices to make this recipe yours. If you like a spicier hummus, add 1 teaspoon chili powder or use a hotter paprika. Or you could buy a spicy dip to pair with the "fries" to pack more of a punch.

Soupe à L'oignon Gratinée
(French Onion Soup)

Chefs de France, France Pavilion

The intricate tile floors and wraparound windows at Chefs de France transport guests straight to France—and so will this dish! It has a smooth, broth-like texture with lots of bread and cheese. You can serve this as two appetizer-sized portions or as a big bowl for one.

SERVES 2

2 tablespoons salted butter
1 tablespoon olive oil
2 cups chopped yellow onion
20 ounces beef broth
1 tablespoon cooking sherry
1 teaspoon dried thyme
1/2 teaspoon ground black pepper
2 slices whole-wheat sandwich bread
1 cup shredded Gruyère cheese

1. In a large pot over medium heat, add butter and olive oil. Once butter is melted, add onion and cook 2 minutes until slightly translucent.
2. Stir in broth, sherry, thyme, and pepper. Bring to a boil, then reduce heat to low and simmer 30 minutes.
3. Place top rack 6" from top of oven and place a baking sheet on rack. Preheat broiler to high.
4. Remove pot from heat and strain through a fine-mesh sieve into two ovenproof bowls. Place 1 bread slice on soup in each bowl. Sprinkle each bowl with 1/2 cup cheese.
5. Place bowls on baking sheet and broil 30 seconds or until cheese is melted but not burnt. Serve immediately.

Mix It Up!

The chefs at Chefs de France use brown sandwich bread to top their French Onion Soup, but you can use whatever bread you prefer: white, sourdough, or French, of course! Each kind of bread will bring a different flavor profile to the dish. Experiment and see what you like best.

Scotch Eggs

Rose & Crown Dining Room, United Kingdom Pavilion

Scotch Eggs sound like something pulled right out of a wild imagination. Hard-boiled eggs wrapped in sausage, rolled in bread crumbs, and deep-fried? It's almost hard to believe this dish is real! Luckily, it is, because the flavors work so well together. The mustard adds much-needed moisture and a tangy flavor to slice through the heartiness of the egg and sausage.

YIELDS 2 SCOTCH EGGS

48 ounces vegetable oil, for frying
1 large egg, beaten
½ cup plain bread crumbs
½ pound ground pork sausage
2 large hard-boiled eggs
1 cup shredded cabbage
2 tablespoons Dijon mustard

1. Preheat oven to 350°F and heat oil in a large pot to 325°F.
2. Put beaten egg in a small bowl and bread crumbs in another small bowl.
3. Divide sausage in half and flatten each half into a disk. Place 1 hard-boiled egg in center of each disk and fold sausage inward to completely envelop egg. Roll each wrapped egg in beaten egg, then roll in bread crumbs.
4. Gently lower eggs into heated oil and fry until golden brown, 3–5 minutes.
5. Remove eggs with a slotted spoon, transfer to a large ungreased ovenproof dish, and bake 10–15 minutes until sausage is cooked through to 160°F.
6. Cut eggs in half and serve two halves each on plates with a bed of cabbage with mustard on the side.

Cooking Technique

Many people are intimidated by deep-frying, but they needn't be. An electric deep fryer is easy to use, as you simply fill it with oil and set the dial to whatever temperature you want it to reach, and it will maintain that temperature. Using a pot on the stove can be just as easy. Use a sturdy candy thermometer that clips to the side of the pot to monitor the temperature.

Pomegranate-Chili Crispy Cauliflower

Spice Road Table, Morocco Pavilion

Disney chefs are very keen to provide food items for people of all dietary lifestyles and restrictions, and Disney Parks certainly have an inexhaustible amount of creative and delicious choices for everyone. This dish is vegetarian.

SERVES 4

For Fried Cauliflower

48 ounces vegetable oil, for frying
1 cup all-purpose flour, divided
1/2 cup almond milk
1 teaspoon salt
1 teaspoon ground black pepper
1 teaspoon garlic powder
1 medium head cauliflower, cored and broken into florets

For Pomegranate Sauce

1/4 cup pure honey
1 tablespoon olive oil
2 tablespoons grenadine
1/4 teaspoon paprika
1/8 teaspoon cayenne pepper
1 teaspoon salt
1 teaspoon garlic powder

For Assembly

4 tablespoons microgreens
4 tablespoons fresh pomegranate arils

1. To make Fried Cauliflower: Heat oil in a large pot over medium heat to 375°F. Line a large plate with paper towels.

2. Place 1/2 cup flour in a small bowl. In a medium bowl, mix remaining 1/2 cup flour, almond milk, salt, pepper, and garlic powder. Dip each cauliflower floret in wet mixture, then dredge in flour. Carefully place 3–5 coated florets in hot oil and fry 3–5 minutes until golden brown. Transfer to prepared plate and repeat with remaining florets.

3. To make Pomegranate Sauce: Mix all sauce ingredients together in a small bowl.

4. To assemble: Remove paper towels from plate. Drizzle Fried Cauliflower generously with Pomegranate Sauce, then sprinkle with microgreens and pomegranate arils. Serve immediately.

Bubble and Squeak

Rose & Crown Dining Room, United Kingdom Pavilion

Disney fans will recognize this dish as mentioned in the classic live action and animated feature *Bedknobs and Broomsticks*, when the Rawlins children ask Miss Eglantine Price to serve them home comfort food, like Bubble and Squeak. One can understand why the Rawlins children loved it, though, because it is a scrumptious dish. Potatoes, bacon, butter—how could you go wrong?

SERVES 6

1 pound russet potatoes, peeled and cubed
2 tablespoons sour cream
2 tablespoons salted butter
1 teaspoon salt
½ teaspoon ground black pepper
3 strips thick-cut bacon
½ medium yellow onion, peeled and diced
1 cup shredded cabbage

1. Bring a medium pot of water to boil over medium-high heat. Add potatoes and boil 15–20 minutes until fork-tender. Drain and return potatoes to pot. Add sour cream, butter, salt, and pepper, then mash with potato masher.

2. Line a medium plate with paper towels. In a small nonstick frying pan over medium heat, cook bacon strips to desired crispiness, 5–8 minutes, then transfer to prepared plate. Once bacon is cool enough to touch, about 5 minutes, crumble into mashed potatoes.

3. Cook onion in pan with bacon grease until tender, 3–5 minutes. Add onion and cabbage to mashed potato mixture. Stir until well combined.

4. Spray a small frying pan with cooking oil and place over medium heat. Scoop about ¼ cup mashed potato mixture into pan. Use a spatula to flatten mixture into a ¼"-thick pancake. Cook 2–4 minutes until browned, then flip and brown opposite side 2–4 minutes. Transfer to a large plate and repeat with remaining mixture. Serve immediately.

Lobster Poutine

Refreshment Port, Canada Pavilion

This dish is perfect for occasions like the Stanley Cup Final, the Grey Cup, or Canada Day! Whenever you want to make this (even if it is any old weeknight), enjoy the decadence of the lobster and the bright notes of the citrus sauce.

SERVES 1

½ cup sour cream
1 tablespoon lemon juice
2 cups frozen French fries, cooked according to package instructions
½ cup lobster bisque soup, cooked according to package instructions
¼ cup cooked lobster chunks

1. Mix sour cream and lemon juice in a small bowl.
2. Pile French fries in a large bowl. Drizzle lobster bisque soup over fries. Spoon on sour cream mixture. Sprinkle with lobster chunks. Serve immediately.

Mozzarella Caprese

Via Napoli Ristorante e Pizzeria, Italy Pavilion

This dish could not be simpler, but it packs a punch in taste and presentation. A basic combination of silky mozzarella cheese and fresh ripe tomatoes pairs so well with the basil and seasonings. A fun addition is a drizzle of balsamic glaze. Andiamo! Get assembling!

SERVES 1

4 (1-ounce) slices fresh mozzarella cheese
3 slices Roma tomato
1 large basil leaf
½ teaspoon salt
¼ teaspoon ground black pepper

Fan out alternating mozzarella and tomato slices on a serving plate. Tuck basil leaf between a slice of cheese and tomato. Sprinkle slices with salt and pepper. Serve.

Canadian Cheddar Cheese Soup

Le Cellier Steakhouse, Canada Pavilion

Canada is situated so far north, most of the year can be bitterly cold with damaging blizzards. Sometimes temperatures plummet so low, it is warmer on Mars than it is in Canada! This soup *feels* so Canadian because it is the perfect warm-up on a cold night. Snuggle up in your favorite hoodie (or "bunnyhug," as some Canadians say) and a knit beanie (or "toque"!) to enjoy this creamy, delightful soup.

SERVES 6

½ pound bacon, diced
2 tablespoons salted butter
1 medium yellow onion, peeled and diced
3 stalks celery, diced
1 cup all-purpose flour
3 cups chicken stock
3 cups whole milk
12 ounces shredded white Cheddar cheese
1 teaspoon salt
½ teaspoon ground black pepper
1 tablespoon Worcestershire sauce
½ cup ginger beer
3 tablespoons chopped green onions

1. In a medium pot over medium heat, cook bacon until brown and crispy, 5–8 minutes. Remove 3 tablespoons bacon and set aside. Add butter, yellow onion, and celery to pot and cook 2 minutes, stirring frequently. Add flour and cook 7 minutes, stirring frequently.
2. Add chicken stock and bring to a boil over high heat, then reduce heat to low and add milk. Simmer 15 minutes, stirring frequently.
3. Turn off heat and add cheese, salt, pepper, Worcestershire sauce, and ginger beer. Stir well and ladle soup into six bowls. Top with reserved bacon and green onions. Serve immediately.

Tomato Soup with French Onion and Bacon Grilled Cheese

Pop Eats!, EPCOT International Festival of the Arts

Disney chefs are hired for their attention to detail, not only with flavor but also with presentation. The tomato soup of this dish is served in a tin can during the festival! Evoking the art of Andy Warhol, Pop Eats! Represents the intersection between realism and whimsy, just like his art.

SERVES 6

For Tomato Soup

- 4 cups diced Roma tomatoes
- 1/2 medium white onion, peeled and chopped
- 4 teaspoons minced fresh garlic
- 2 cups chicken stock
- 2 tablespoons salted butter
- 2 tablespoons all-purpose flour
- 2 teaspoons salt
- 2 teaspoons granulated sugar
- 1 tablespoon Italian seasoning
- 6 small sprigs fresh parsley, divided

1. To make Tomato Soup: In a large pot over medium heat, add tomatoes, onion, garlic and stock. Cook 20 minutes. Pour cooked tomato mixture into a blender (in batches if needed) or use an immersion blender to blend until smooth.

2. In a separate large pot over medium heat, add butter and flour. Stir and cook 4 minutes to make a roux. Add tomato mixture to roux one ladle at a time, whisking between each addition until all soup has been added. Add salt, sugar, and Italian seasoning. Stir until well combined. Ladle into six serving cups and garnish each with 1 small sprig parsley. Leftovers can be stored up to 5 days in a sealed container in the refrigerator.

For Sandwiches

7 tablespoons salted butter, softened, divided
3 medium yellow onions, peeled and sliced
3 tablespoons bacon bits
3 cups shredded Gruyère cheese
12 slices whole-grain bread

3. To make Sandwiches: Melt 1 tablespoon butter in a large nonstick pan over medium heat and add onions. Stir until onions are browned and soft, 5–8 minutes. Add bacon bits and cheese. Stir to melt and combine.

4. Spread remaining butter on one side of each bread slice. Place 6 bread slices butter-side down and scoop onion mixture on bread, then top with remaining bread slices (butter-side up). Grill buttered sides of bread 3–5 minutes in same pan in batches until all are grilled.

5. Remove sandwiches from pan, slice in half, then serve alongside Tomato Soup.

Serving Suggestion

If you want to serve your soup in a can at home, carefully remove the lid with a can opener and thoroughly clean the can before adding soup. Pop Eats! serves its soup in a short, fat can, but you can use whatever can size you have available.

Watermelon Salad

The juicy watermelon in this recipe pairs so well with the vinegary flavor of the pickled onions, rounded out by the unique flavor of the balsamic glaze and the brightness of the greens. It truly is a bouquet of flavors and textures!

SERVES 4

For Pickled Onions

1 medium red onion, peeled and sliced thin
3/4 cup apple cider vinegar
1 teaspoon salt
1/4 cup water
2 tablespoons granulated sugar
1 tablespoon pure honey

For Balsamic Glaze

1 cup balsamic vinegar
1/4 cup light brown sugar

For Watermelon Salad

4 cups watermelon cubes
2 cups fresh arugula
1 cup feta cheese crumbles

1. To make Pickled Onions: Place sliced onion in a pint Mason jar. Set aside. In a small saucepan over medium heat, add apple cider vinegar, salt, water, sugar, and honey. Bring to a boil, reduce heat to low, and simmer 3 minutes. Pour over onion in jar and refrigerate at least 2 hours up to overnight.

2. To make Balsamic Glaze: Add balsamic vinegar and brown sugar to a small saucepan over medium heat. Stir frequently, bring to a boil, then reduce heat to low. Simmer 8–10 minutes until only 1/4 cup liquid remains. Pour into a small sealable container and refrigerate until chilled, about 1 hour.

3. To make Watermelon Salad: Divide watermelon cubes among four serving plates. Top each with 1/2 cup arugula, 1/4 cup feta, and 2 tablespoons Pickled Onions. Drizzle with Balsamic Glaze. Serve immediately. Leftover Pickled Onions and Balsamic Glaze can be kept covered in the refrigerator up to 1 month.

Simplification Hack

If you are trying to make this for an event (or might be pressed for time at dinner), make the Pickled Onions ahead of time, then simply assemble the salad before serving.

Grilled Baby Vegetables

Flavor Full Kitchen, EPCOT International Flower & Garden Festival

A delicious vegan appetizer made of yummy vegetables. The combination of hummus and red pepper coulis creates a parade of new flavors in your mouth.

SERVES 4

1 tablespoon olive oil
1 medium red bell
   pepper, seeded and
   sliced
1/2 medium yellow onion,
   peeled and chopped
1/2 cup vegan white
   cooking wine
1/2 cup vegetable stock
1 tablespoon vegetable
   oil
1 medium zucchini,
   sliced lengthwise into
   4 pieces
1 medium yellow squash,
   halved and sliced
   lengthwise into
   4 pieces
4 medium cherry
   tomatoes
1 large carrot, peeled and
   sliced on a diagonal
   into 4 pieces
1 teaspoon salt
1/2 teaspoon ground black
   pepper
4 tablespoons plain
   hummus

1. Heat olive oil in a large nonstick pan over medium heat. Add red pepper and onion. Stir and cook until soft and slightly charred, 3–5 minutes. Remove from heat and carefully pour mixture into a blender. Add wine and vegetable stock and blend until smooth. Pour into a container, cover, and refrigerate 2 hours.

2. Rub vegetables with oil and sprinkle with salt and black pepper. Grill over medium-high heat until soft and slightly charred, 5–7 minutes. (If you don't have a grill, heat vegetable oil in a clean large nonstick pan over medium heat. Add zucchini, squash, cherry tomatoes, and carrot. Sprinkle with salt and black pepper. Stir and cook 5–7 minutes until vegetables are soft and slightly charred.)

3. Scoop 1 tablespoon hummus and red pepper coulis onto each of four medium plates. Add 1 piece of each vegetable. Serve immediately.

Grilled Street Corn on the Cob

Trowel & Trellis, EPCOT International Flower & Garden Festival

This Grilled Street Corn on the Cob is a festival favorite and returns year after year to satiate hungry parkgoers looking for a fresh bite. The buttery margarine and fresh herbs on grilled corn taste like summer in your hand.

SERVES 6

1 cup margarine,
  softened
1 tablespoon lemon juice
1 teaspoon minced fresh
  garlic
1 teaspoon chopped
  fresh parsley
1 teaspoon chopped
  fresh chives
1 teaspoon salt
6 medium ears corn,
  shucked
1 cup crumbled vegan
  cotija cheese

1. Preheat grill or grill pan to 350°F.
2. Combine margarine, lemon juice, garlic, parsley, chives, and salt in a small bowl. Spread half of mixture over corncobs. Place on grill and close lid. Cook 10 minutes, turning corn often, or until margarine is melted and corn is bright yellow with some charring.
3. Remove corn to a large plate and smear with remaining margarine mixture while corn is still hot. Sprinkle cotija over corn and serve immediately.

CHAPTER 4

Entrées

Unlike the other Parks at the Walt Disney World Resort, EPCOT sometimes offers an "after 4 p.m." ticket so people can come for dinner in the evening. Each of the World Showcase pavilions has one (sometimes more!) table-service restaurant that goes over-the-top in showcasing its cultural palate.

With this cookbook, you can visit the flavors of EPCOT in the comfort of your own home. Pick a country and make a recipe from that location in this chapter. Be sure to pair it with a great drink from Chapter 6! For example, try pairing the Carne Asada with a La Cava Avocado, or the Fish and Chips with a Pimm's Cup. And don't forget the ambiance—some colorful decorations and festive dinnerware will go a long way toward feeling as though you've stepped into a different country. Or cue up the classic EPCOT nighttime spectacular IllumiNations on *YouTube* and snuggle into some comfy blankets for a more laid-back dinner with the family. However you want to enjoy these meals, celebrate the cultures and traditions that brought them to your table. The world is a huge place. But also, it's a small world after all.

Carne Asada

San Angel Inn Restaurante, Mexico Pavilion

Carne Asada is one of the most popular dishes served at San Angel Inn Restaurante—for good reason. The flavorful and sweet marinade sets this steak apart. Of course, it can be quite a hit to the wallet too! Enjoy the savings of making this at home. You can buy quick Mexican rice from the grocery store to make as a side, as well as some black beans seasoned with salt, pepper, and cilantro.

SERVES 2

1 (16-ounce) New York strip steak, halved
3 teaspoons minced fresh garlic
¼ cup lime juice
¼ cup olive oil
1 teaspoon ancho chili powder
1 teaspoon salt
½ teaspoon ground black pepper
4 tablespoons agave syrup

1. Place steak in a large zip-top bag. Add remaining ingredients to bag. Seal bag and mix well, then refrigerate 1 hour.
2. Preheat grill to 350°F. Cook until desired temperature, about 8–10 minutes per side to 155°F for medium doneness. Remove from grill and allow to rest on a cutting board 5 minutes before slicing and serving.

EPCOT Park Tip

If you get the chance to dine at San Angel Inn Restaurante, be sure to ask to sit near the water's edge. The attraction Gran Fiesta Tour Starring the Three Caballeros flows right past the restaurant, and diners sitting there can enjoy the ambiance. It is akin to Blue Bayou Restaurant at Disneyland, where diners are seated inside the Pirates of the Caribbean attraction.

Norwegian Meatballs

Akershus Royal Banquet Hall, Norway Pavilion

Most non-Scandinavians are more familiar with Swedish meatballs than Norwegian meatballs. We have IKEA to thank for that! While both meatballs are quite similar, the main difference is the shape. Swedish meatballs are golf ball–sized and round, while Norwegian meatballs are a bit larger and flatter. However you shape them, these meatballs are moist and flavorful. Paired with a cream sauce and lingonberry jam, these meatballs offer a savory-and-sweet party in your mouth.

SERVES 6

For Meatballs

1 pound lean ground beef
1/2 pound ground pork
1/2 cup plain bread crumbs
1/4 cup finely diced yellow onion
1 teaspoon salt
1 teaspoon granulated sugar
1/4 teaspoon ground ginger
1/4 teaspoon ground nutmeg
1/4 teaspoon ground allspice
1/2 teaspoon ground black pepper
1 large egg
1/2 cup whole milk

1. To make Meatballs: Preheat oven to 400°F. Place a wire cooling rack on a baking sheet and spray rack with nonstick cooking spray.
2. In a large bowl, mix all Meatballs ingredients together until well combined.
3. Use a spoon or cookie scoop to scoop into balls approximately 1/4 cup in size. Roll mixture and then slightly flatten. Place on prepared cooling rack, leaving a small amount of space between Meatballs.
4. Bake 15–20 minutes until internal temperature reaches 160°F.

For Cream Sauce

2 tablespoons salted butter
3 tablespoons all-purpose flour
1¾ cups beef broth
¼ cup heavy whipping cream
½ teaspoon salt
½ teaspoon ground black pepper

For Assembly

1 cup lingonberry jam
6 cups prepared russet mashed potatoes

5. To make Cream Sauce: In a small saucepan over medium heat, melt butter. Add flour and stir. Cook 1 minute. Slowly add beef broth while whisking vigorously. Allow to come to a boil, then reduce heat to low and simmer 1 minute while whisking. Remove from heat and stir in cream, salt, and pepper.

6. To assemble: Divide mashed potatoes among six serving bowls or deep plates. Top each serving with 3 Meatballs. Pile lingonberry jam on top and drizzle all over with Cream Sauce. Serve immediately.

Salt and Pepper Shrimp with Spinach Noodles

Nine Dragons Restaurant, China Pavilion

The spinach noodles lend an original flavor (and color!) to this dish. Spinach noodles may not be sold at big-box stores, but you can locate them at most regular grocery stores or specialty stores. Of course, if you prefer plain linguine, that works just as well! Play around with different noodle varieties.

SERVES 2

1 cup plus 1 teaspoon vegetable oil, divided
20 large frozen cooked, tail-on shrimp
1 cup cornstarch
2 teaspoons ground black pepper
1 teaspoon coarse sea salt
1 small white onion, peeled and sliced into strips
1/2 medium red bell pepper, seeded and sliced into strips
1 teaspoon minced fresh garlic
1 teaspoon ginger paste
1/2 teaspoon red pepper flakes
1/4 cup low-sodium soy sauce
3 tablespoons light brown sugar
1/2 pound cooked spinach linguine
1/4 cup chopped fresh cilantro

1. Heat 1 cup oil in a wok or large skillet over medium heat to 375°F. Line a large plate with paper towels.

2. Soak frozen shrimp in room-temperature water 5 minutes. Drain and pat dry with paper towels.

3. Mix cornstarch, black pepper, and salt together in a small shallow bowl and coat shrimp in mixture, shaking off excess. Carefully slide 5 shrimp into hot oil and cook 1–2 minutes until lightly fried. Transfer to prepared plate and repeat with remaining shrimp. Carefully discard hot oil once cooled and clean wok.

4. Return wok to stove over medium heat and add remaining 1 teaspoon oil, onion, and bell pepper. Cook over medium heat 1 minute. Add garlic, ginger paste, and red pepper flakes. Cook 1 minute. Add soy sauce and brown sugar. Bring to a boil, then reduce heat to low and simmer 3 minutes, stirring occasionally. Remove from heat.

5. Toss spinach linguine in sauce in wok. Divide between two bowls and top each bowl with 10 shrimp and 2 tablespoons cilantro. Serve immediately.

Honey Sesame Chicken

Nine Dragons Restaurant, China Pavilion

Honey Sesame Chicken is a staple of Chinese takeout boxes, but did you know it is simple to make at home? This recipe serves just one person, but if you are gathering the family around, just add more chicken breasts and multiply the batter and coating. Banana Cheesecake Egg Rolls (see recipe in Chapter 5) makes a nice dessert with this meal.

SERVES 1

For Chicken

48 ounces vegetable oil, for frying
1 teaspoon salt
½ teaspoon ground black pepper
1 large boneless, skinless chicken breast, diced into 1" cubes
1 large egg
½ cup all-purpose flour
¼ cup cornstarch
½ teaspoon baking powder
1 tablespoon vegetable oil
½ cup cold water

For Honey Coating

½ cup pure honey
1 teaspoon sesame oil
½ teaspoon salt
1 tablespoon white sesame seeds
1 tablespoon diced green onions

1. To make Chicken: Heat 48 ounces oil in a large pot over medium heat to 325°F. Line a large plate with paper towels.
2. Sprinkle salt and pepper over chicken cubes. In a large bowl, mix together egg, flour, cornstarch, baking powder, 1 tablespoon oil, and water. Place chicken cubes in batter and coat.
3. Carefully transfer chicken cubes from batter to hot oil and fry 5 minutes, or until chicken reaches an internal temperature of 165°F and is no longer pink inside. Transfer to prepared plate.
4. To make Honey Coating: In a small saucepan or wok over medium heat, heat honey, sesame oil, and salt until warm, 2–3 minutes. Add Chicken and toss to coat. Sprinkle with sesame seeds and green onions and serve.

Simplification Hack

Rice pairs great with this meal and can be made easily in a rice cooker or easily and quickly if you opt for instant rice or microwavable rice cups.

Mole Poblano

San Angel Inn Restaurante, Mexico Pavilion

Mole has a long and wonderful history that began in the Oaxaca and Puebla regions of Mexico. Mole paste, nuts, seasonings, and peppers come together to create a complex flavor. But what often sets mole apart from other sauces is its most unusual ingredient: cocoa. You can certainly taste hints of chocolate that are distinctly bitter and sweet.

SERVES 2

2 (6-ounce) boneless, skinless chicken breasts

2 teaspoons salt

2 teaspoons ground black pepper

$2/3$ cup plus 2 tablespoons chicken stock, divided, plus extra as needed

3 tablespoons mole paste

$1/2$ medium poblano pepper, seeded and sliced into strips

2 teaspoons white sesame seeds

2 tablespoons sliced almonds

6 (6") corn tortillas

1. Preheat grill to 350°F.

2. Season chicken breasts on both sides with salt and black pepper. Grill until internal temperature reaches 165°F, 9–10 minutes. Remove from grill and allow to rest 5 minutes before slicing.

3. Mix $2/3$ cup chicken stock with mole paste in a small saucepan over medium heat. Bring to a boil, then reduce heat to low and simmer 4 minutes. If sauce is too thick, add 1 tablespoon extra chicken stock at a time until desired consistency.

4. In a separate small saucepan, add remaining 2 tablespoons chicken stock and poblano pepper. Cook and stir 5–10 minutes over medium heat until pepper is soft and liquid is gone.

5. In a blender, add mole sauce and cooked pepper. Blend until smooth.

6. To assemble, slice chicken breasts into $1/2$" strips, cutting against the grain. Pour mole sauce over chicken and sprinkle with sesame seeds and almonds. Wrap tortillas in damp paper towels and microwave 30 seconds. Serve alongside chicken.

Schnitzel

Biergarten Restaurant, Germany Pavilion

Pork schnitzel is just one of the many ways you can prepare this crispy German meal. Other proteins you could use include veal, chicken, mutton, beef, and turkey. And depending on what part of the world you are in, maybe your most easily accessible meat is buffalo, elk, caribou, or something else entirely! Whatever meat you choose, this is a crunchy main dish that's hard not to love. Serve alongside noodles and sausages.

SERVES 4

48 ounces vegetable oil, for frying
1/2 cup all-purpose flour
2 large eggs, beaten
1 cup plain bread crumbs
4 (6-ounce) boneless pork chops
1 tablespoon salt
1 tablespoon ground black pepper

1. Heat oil in a pot over medium heat to 350°F. Line a large plate with paper towels.
2. Place flour in a shallow dish. Pour eggs into a second shallow dish. Add bread crumbs to a third shallow dish.
3. Pound pork chops to 1/4" thickness and sprinkle with salt and pepper on each side. Dip chops one at a time in flour, then eggs, then bread crumbs. Shake off any excess crumbs.
4. Gently lower 1 pork chop into hot oil. Fry 2–3 minutes or until golden brown and internal temperature reaches 145°F. Transfer to prepared plate and repeat with remaining chops. Serve immediately.

Sliced Texas Beef Brisket Sandwiches

Regal Eagle Smokehouse, The American Adventure Pavilion

While most people do not own a pellet smoker (which is typically used in cooking brisket), you can easily turn your propane or charcoal grill into a smoker. See Chapter 2 to learn more!

SERVES 4

For Brisket
1/4 cup salt
1/4 cup ground black pepper
1 (6-pound) beef brisket

For Garlic Texas Toast
4 tablespoons salted butter, softened
2 teaspoons garlic powder
1 teaspoon coarse salt
2 teaspoons Italian seasoning
8 slices Texas Toast
4 tablespoons sweet barbecue sauce

1. To make Brisket: Place 6 cups hickory wood chips in a large bowl and cover with water. Allow to soak 30 minutes.
2. Set up smoker box in grill (see Chapter 2). Scoop 1/2 cup wood chips into smoker box and ignite just the heating element under smoker box. Reduce heat to low.
3. Mix salt and pepper in a small bowl. Rub all over brisket. Place brisket as far as possible from smoker box, over turned-off heating elements. Close grill lid.
4. Smoke 8–10 hours until internal temperature reaches 190°F. Each hour, add 1/4–1/2 cup wood chips to smoker box. Smoke should be consistently filling grill. Remove brisket from grill and transfer to a cutting board. Allow to rest 30 minutes.
5. To make Garlic Texas Toast: Mix butter, garlic powder, salt, and Italian seasoning in a small bowl. Toast bread in toaster to preferred doneness and spread one side of each piece with butter mixture.
6. Slice brisket with a sharp knife across the grain into very thin slices. Pile onto 4 Garlic Texas Toast slices (with butter mixture inside), drizzle with barbecue sauce, and top with remaining Garlic Texas Toast. Serve immediately.

Margherita Pizzas

Via Napoli Ristorante e Pizzeria, Italy Pavilion

Pizza at Via Napoli Ristorante e Pizzeria is baked unlike at any other restaurant—in volcano-inspired ovens! Each of the three pizza ovens is named after an Italian volcano, letting guests know these ovens are *hot*. How hot? Like 700°F hot. Wood inside burns ultra hot to bake pizzas quickly, creating thin and crispy crust. Preheating a baking sheet helps raise the temperature of the crust faster in your home oven.

YIELDS 2 (12") PIZZAS

1 cup warm water (110°F)
1 teaspoon rapid-rise yeast
1 teaspoon olive oil
2¼ cups all-purpose flour
1 cup tomato sauce
2 (16-ounce) packages fresh mozzarella cheese slices
16 fresh basil leaves

1. In a large bowl, mix warm water, yeast, olive oil, and flour with your hands until just combined and dough is shaggy. Cover with a clean towel and let sit 15 minutes.
2. Grease a separate large bowl with oil.
3. After 15 minutes, knead dough by hand 3 minutes or until dough is well combined and soft. Cut into two equal-sized pieces and place each piece in a prepared bowl. Cover with a tea towel. Let rise in a warm place (such as near a stove) 1 hour.
4. Place a baking sheet in oven and preheat oven to 550°F.
5. Turn each dough ball out onto a clean surface. Coat your hands in olive oil and carefully push each ball into a flat, round crust.

(continued on next page)

6. Spread sauce onto crusts, leaving $\frac{1}{2}$" from the edges clean. Top with mozzarella and basil.

7. Carefully remove baking sheet from oven and place 1 pizza on sheet. Return to oven and bake 5–7 minutes until crust is browned and cheese is melted. Repeat with second pizza. Slice and serve immediately.

Cooking Technique

Another way to cook pizza at home is to grill it. Preheat a pizza stone on a propane or charcoal grill on high heat and add your pizza. Every couple of minutes, rotate the pizza so each side cooks evenly. Keep a close eye on it because it will cook quickly!

Tri-Colored Tortellini

Primavera Kitchen, EPCOT International Flower & Garden Festival

Primavera Kitchen is an outdoor booth you can find around the Italy Pavilion during the EPCOT International Flower & Garden Festival held each year. Since it has a rotating menu, this dish may or may not be available on your next trip. Luckily, you can make this at home anytime to enjoy these delicious and bright flavors. Using fresh sage adds depth and fragrance. And while Primavera Kitchen uses prepackaged tortellini in this dish, feel free to make fresh tortellini at home!

SERVES 4

- 3½ cups chicken stock
- 2 tablespoons clarified butter
- 3 tablespoons all-purpose flour
- 30 fresh sage leaves
- 1 (20-ounce) bag tri-color tortellini
- 4 tablespoons grated Parmesan cheese

1. In a medium saucepan over medium-high heat, heat chicken stock until hot and simmering, about 3 minutes. Remove from heat.
2. In a separate medium saucepan over medium heat, melt butter. Add flour and stir to combine. Cook 2 minutes, stirring constantly, to make a roux. Carefully ladle 3 cups hot chicken stock into roux, whisking continuously.
3. Reduce heat to low. Add sage leaves and simmer 30 minutes or until sauce is thickened slightly. Use reserved stock if sauce gets too thick. Pour sauce through a sieve.
4. Cook tortellini according to package instructions. Spoon onto four serving plates, pour on sauce, and top with Parmesan. Serve immediately.

North Carolina Chopped Smoked Pork Butt

Regal Eagle Smokehouse, The American Adventure Pavilion

North Carolina barbeque sauce is thin and non-tomato-based, and has a tart flavor lent from the apple cider vinegar. It's used to lock moisture into the meat during cooking for pull-apart pork no one can resist.

SERVES 4

2 cups apple cider vinegar
1/2 cup light brown sugar
1/4 cup ketchup
1/2 teaspoon cayenne pepper
1/4 teaspoon chili powder
1/2 teaspoon ground black pepper
1 teaspoon salt
1 (3-pound) bone-in pork butt
4 tablespoons sweet barbecue sauce
4 slices Garlic Texas Toast (see Sliced Texas Beef Brisket Sandwiches recipe in this chapter)

1. Place 6 cups hickory wood chips in a large bowl and cover with water. Allow to soak 30 minutes.

2. In a small saucepan over medium heat, combine apple cider vinegar, brown sugar, ketchup, cayenne pepper, chili powder, black pepper, and salt. Bring to a boil, then remove from heat. Pour sauce into a small bowl or jar, reserving 1/4 cup.

3. Set up smoker box in grill (see Chapter 2). Scoop 1/2 cup wood chips into smoker box and ignite just the heating element under smoker box. Reduce heat to low. Place pork butt as far as possible from smoker box, over turned-off heating elements, and brush with sauce. Close grill lid.

4. Smoke 8–10 hours until internal temperature reaches 145°F. Each hour, add 1/4–1/2 cup wood chips to smoker box. Smoke should be consistently filling grill. Each hour also generously brush more vinegar sauce over pork. Remove pork butt from grill and transfer to a cutting board. Allow to rest 30 minutes.

5. Shred pork with two forks and pile onto four plates. Brush on reserved vinegar sauce. Drizzle with barbecue sauce. Serve with Garlic Texas Toast.

Lemon Chicken Tagine

Spice Road Table, Morocco Pavilion

For this recipe, you can use fresh lemons. If you want to preserve your own lemons, just cut fresh lemons into quarters and sprinkle each quarter with 1 tablespoon kosher salt. Pack the lemon quarters into a large jar, pushing down to squeeze juices out. Add extra lemon juice so lemons are covered and sprinkle with extra kosher salt. Seal the jar and allow to sit at room temperature 3 days, then refrigerate 3 weeks (up to 6 months), shaking the jar periodically to mix. Rinse lemons before using.

SERVES 6

- 1 (5–7 pound) whole skin-on chicken, broken down into legs, wings, breasts, and thighs
- 1 cup warm water
- 1 teaspoon saffron threads
- 3 tablespoons olive oil
- 1 yellow onion, peeled and diced
- 3 teaspoons minced fresh garlic
- 2 teaspoons minced fresh ginger
- 1 teaspoon ground turmeric
- 1 teaspoon paprika
- 1 teaspoon ground coriander
- 1 teaspoon salt
- 2 teaspoons dried cilantro
- Juice of 1 large preserved lemon
- ¼ cup green olives

1. Preheat oven to 350°F.
2. In a large nonstick pan over medium-high heat, place all chicken pieces skin-side down and sear until skin is brown, 2–5 minutes. Remove from heat and set aside.
3. Prepare saffron water by mixing warm water and saffron threads in a small bowl. Allow to sit 10 minutes.
4. Place a 3-ounce tagine over medium heat. Add olive oil and onion and cook 5 minutes, stirring occasionally. Add garlic and cook 5 minutes more.
5. Add remaining seasonings and 3 tablespoons saffron water. Arrange chicken in a single layer skin-side up over onion. Squeeze lemon juice over chicken and add olives. Close lid and cook 1½ hours until chicken is tender and internal temperature reaches 165°F. Serve.

Cooking Technique

While tagines can easily be acquired at online stores, they can be pricey. If you don't have one, feel free to use a Dutch oven or other sturdy heatproof pot with a lid.

BBQ Jackfruit Burgers

Regal Eagle Smokehouse, The American Adventure Pavilion

Disney's faux meat brand of choice is Impossible Foods, but these products can be difficult to find in grocery stores. Some alternatives include Beyond Meat, Lightlife, and Pure Farmland. Serve with French fries, topped with a little American flag for the full EPCOT experience.

SERVES 2

- 1 (20-ounce) can jackfruit in brine, drained and cored
- 1 cup water
- 1 cup vegan barbecue sauce
- 2 (4-ounce) Impossible Burger patties
- ½ teaspoon salt
- ¼ teaspoon ground black pepper
- 1 tablespoon vegan margarine
- 4 slices Garlic Texas Toast (see Sliced Texas Beef Brisket Sandwiches in this chapter; substitute vegan butter)
- ½ cup shredded iceberg lettuce
- 2 large slices beefsteak tomato
- 2 tablespoons vegan mayonnaise
- 2 frozen onion rings, cooked according to package instructions

1. Place jackfruit and water in the pot of an electric pressure cooker. Seal lid and cook on high pressure 5 minutes. Allow to naturally release pressure, then drain jackfruit and return jackfruit to pressure cooker on the sauté setting. Break up pieces with two forks, add barbecue sauce, and sauté 2–4 minutes until sauce and jackfruit are warmed through. Set pot to warm until ready to serve.

2. Sprinkle burger patties with salt and pepper on each side and cook in a large nonstick pan over medium heat until brown and warmed through, about 2–3 minutes per side.

3. Spread margarine over one side of toast slices with margarine side inward. On each of 2 slices, pile ¼ cup lettuce, 1 tomato slice, 1 patty, and half of jackfruit. Spread mayonnaise on one side of remaining toast slices and place on top of jackfruit. Top each sandwich with 1 onion ring and serve.

Mix It Up!

If you would rather have traditional ground beef for this burger instead of an Impossible Burger, just substitute ground beef patties. The taste will be almost the same!

Tonkotsu (Pork) Ramen

Katsura Grill, Japan Pavilion

Many Americans think of ramen as a "poor college student" meal that consists of noodles from a packet seasoned with some freeze-dried stock. However, ramen is an incredibly diverse Japanese dish that can be as decadent as you want it to be. It is infinitely customizable; whatever toppings you dream up can be added to this dish. Common additions are hard-boiled eggs, vegetables, and fish cakes.

SERVES 2

2 teaspoons sesame oil
1 tablespoon minced fresh ginger
3 tablespoons soy sauce
2 tablespoons mirin
4 cups chicken stock
1 teaspoon dashi granules
2 tablespoons salted butter, divided
2 teaspoons salt
1 teaspoon ground black pepper
2 (3-ounce) thin-sliced pork chops
1/2 cup drained canned corn
1 cup baby broccoli
2 (3-ounce) blocks ramen noodles, cooked according to package instructions

1. Pour sesame oil into a medium pot over medium-high heat. Add ginger, soy sauce, mirin, chicken stock, and dashi granules. Bring to a boil, then reduce heat to low and simmer 20 minutes to allow flavors to blend.

2. Melt 1 tablespoon butter in a medium nonstick pan over medium heat. Salt and pepper both sides of pork chops and cook in buttered pan until browned and internal temperature reaches 145°F. Set chops aside.

3. Melt remaining butter in same pan and add corn. Heat until warmed and starting to char, about 3–5 minutes.

4. Bring 1" water to a boil in a medium pot over medium heat and add a steamer basket above it. Add baby broccoli, cover pot, and steam 3–5 minutes until baby broccoli is bright green and tender.

5. Scoop cooked ramen noodles into two medium bowls. Ladle in stock. Slice pork chops and place on noodles. Place corn on noodles. Place baby broccoli on corn. Serve immediately with chopsticks and large spoons.

Nihonbashi

Teppan Edo, Japan Pavilion

Have you ever been to a teppanyaki restaurant, like Benihana? Teppan Edo offers a similar experience but with a Disney touch, of course. Guests watch chefs cook their meal right at their table on a hot huge griddle. Re-create this experience in your own home with this recipe—just don't make any fireballs in your kitchen!

SERVES 2

1/2 cup soy sauce

4 tablespoons apple cider vinegar

2 tablespoons granulated sugar

1 tablespoon minced fresh ginger

1 tablespoon minced fresh garlic

2 1/2 teaspoons ground black pepper, divided

2 teaspoons salt, divided

1 (8-ounce) New York strip steak

4 tablespoons salted butter, divided

1 (6-ounce) boneless, skinless chicken breast

1 medium zucchini, halved lengthwise and sliced into half-moons

1/2 medium yellow onion, peeled and sliced

1/4 pound udon noodles, cooked

1. Combine soy sauce, apple cider vinegar, sugar, ginger, garlic, and 1 teaspoon pepper in a medium microwave-safe bowl. Microwave on high 1 minute, stir, and microwave 1 minute more. Set aside.

2. Sprinkle 1 teaspoon salt and 1/2 teaspoon pepper on steak. Melt 1 tablespoon butter in a large nonstick pan over medium heat. Cook steak 3–5 minutes, flipping halfway through, until it reaches an internal temperature of 145°F. Transfer steak to a plate.

3. Melt 1 tablespoon butter in same pan over medium heat. Cook chicken 4–6 minutes, flipping halfway through, until it reaches an internal temperature of 165°F. Transfer chicken to plate with steak.

4. Melt remaining 2 tablespoons butter in same pan over medium heat. Sprinkle remaining 1 teaspoon salt and 1 teaspoon pepper over zucchini and onion. Cook until fork-tender and slightly charred, 5–7 minutes.

5. Cut steak and chicken into bite-sized chunks and add to vegetables in pan. Add 1/4 cup sauce and stir to combine.

6. Divide between two large plates. Add cooked udon noodles to pan and add remaining sauce. Toss to combine and divide between plates. Serve immediately.

Boeuf Bourguignon

Chefs de France, France Pavilion

This dish is well known for its appearance in the movie *Julie & Julia*, where character Julie Powell blogs her way through Julia Child's cookbook, *Mastering the Art of French Cooking*. Designed specifically to be easy and quick, this version of a Boeuf Bourguignon is done in an electric pressure cooker.

SERVES 2

2 tablespoons olive oil, divided
1 (1-pound) beef chuck tender roast, cut into 6 chunks
1 tablespoon salt
1 tablespoon ground black pepper
1 cup beef broth
1 cup red cooking wine
2 teaspoons minced fresh garlic
3 large carrots, peeled and cut into 1" chunks on a diagonal
1 cup frozen pearl onions
3 tablespoons salted butter, divided
2 tablespoons cornstarch
3 tablespoons cold water
$\frac{1}{2}$ pound linguine, cooked
1 tablespoon chopped fresh chives

1. In the pot of an electric pressure cooker, add 1 tablespoon olive oil and press the Sauté button. Allow pot to heat up 5 minutes.

2. Season beef chunks on all sides with salt and pepper. Once pot is hot, sear 3 chunks about 1 minute on each side until browned. Transfer to a large plate. Add remaining olive oil to pot and sear remaining beef chunks. Transfer to plate.

3. Add beef broth and wine to pot and scrape all meat bits off the bottom. Add garlic, carrots, and onions. Return meat to pot. Seal lid and valve and set to pressure cook 1 hour to internal meat temperature of 160°F.

4. Release pressure. Strain contents, retaining juice. Press Sauté again on pot and add 1 tablespoon butter. Pour in 1½ cups reserved juice. Combine cornstarch and water in a small cup and stir well. Gradually pour mixture into pot while whisking vigorously. Continue to whisk frequently and sauté 5 minutes.

5. Toss remaining 2 tablespoons butter with hot cooked linguine and scoop onto one half of two wide, shallow bowls. Place 3 meat chunks onto the other side of each bowl. Top meat with carrots and onions. Drizzle meat with gravy from pot and sprinkle with chives. Serve immediately.

Ribeye Steak, USDA Prime

Le Cellier Steakhouse, Canada Pavilion

Few pleasures in life match that of enjoying a delicious fillet of steak. The secret to an incredible steak is the quality of cut. The price tag will be worth it!

SERVES 1

1 (3/4-pound) USDA Prime ribeye steak
1 teaspoon flaky salt
2 teaspoons Montreal steak seasoning
2 tablespoons salted butter
1/4 cup French-fried onions

1. Heat a large nonstick pan over high heat. Season steak with salt and steak seasoning on all sides. Once pan is smoking, add butter, allow to melt, then add steak. Sear steak, cooking all sides, to preferred doneness (medium doneness will be an internal temperature of 145°F, 5–7 minutes).
2. Remove from pan and allow to rest on a cutting board or plate 10 minutes, then transfer steak to a serving plate and top with onions. Serve immediately.

Serving Suggestion

If you'd rather have fresh onion straws to top your steak, follow these simple instructions. Slice 1/4 yellow onion into very thin strips, place in a medium bowl, and cover with buttermilk. Mix 1/4 cup all-purpose flour, 1 teaspoon salt, and 1/2 teaspoon ground black pepper in a separate medium bowl. Dredge onion strings in flour mixture and shake off excess. Fry in 350°F oil over medium-high heat 1–2 minutes until crispy and drain on a paper towel–lined plate.

Fish and Chips

Nothing could be more British than Fish and Chips! Made with fresh cod, these crispy fried fishes and hearty helping of fries truly transport you to the land of the Union Jack. In England, Fish and Chips are often served in a newsprint cone to carry in one hand, with a tiny wooden fork to eat it with. In that same spirit, Yorkshire County Fish Shop lines its Fish and Chips trays with news-printed parchment paper. Don't forget the lemon wedges and tartar sauce and maybe even a shake of malt vinegar on top!

SERVES 2

½ cup all-purpose flour, divided
¼ cup cornstarch
½ cup ginger ale
48 ounces vegetable oil, for frying
4 (7-ounce) pieces fresh cod, sliced ½" thick
1 teaspoon salt
½ teaspoon ground black pepper
4 cups frozen French fries, cooked according to package instructions
4 tablespoons tartar sauce
1 medium lemon, quartered

1. In a medium bowl, mix together ¼ cup flour, cornstarch, and ginger ale. Refrigerate 30 minutes.
2. Heat oil in a medium pot over medium heat to 350°F. Line a large plate with paper towels.
3. Dry fish pieces thoroughly with a paper towel, then season with salt and pepper on each side. Dredge fish in remaining ¼ cup flour, shaking off excess, then dip in chilled batter, allowing excess to drip off back into bowl.
4. Carefully lower fish into hot oil, frying 2 pieces at a time. Turning frequently, fry 5–8 minutes until internal temperature reaches 145°F and batter is golden brown. Transfer to prepared plate.
5. Serve immediately on top of French fries, alongside tartar sauce and lemon wedges.

Deconstructed BLTs

The Deconstructed Dish, EPCOT International Festival of the Arts

You may be thinking that this is just two plates with a piece of bacon, lettuce, and tomato sitting on them. But no! EPCOT International Festival of the Arts is well known for taking food up a notch. This dish is a deconstructed BLT in its *very best* form. The "bacon" is crisp pork belly, the "tomato" is a homemade tomato jam, and a soft-poached egg is thrown in for good measure. If that doesn't sound like the best BLT you've ever heard of, I don't know what is!

SERVES 2

2 Roma tomatoes, diced
¹⁄₂ cup granulated sugar
1 tablespoon lime juice
2 teaspoons minced fresh ginger
¹⁄₂ teaspoon ground cumin
¹⁄₄ teaspoon ground cinnamon
³⁄₄ teaspoon salt, divided
1 tablespoon canned diced jalapeños
1 tablespoon olive oil
2 (1" × 3") chunks pork belly
2 large eggs
1 tablespoon white wine vinegar
¹⁄₄ teaspoon ground black pepper
1 slice brioche bread

1. In a medium saucepan over medium heat, combine tomatoes, sugar, lime juice, ginger, cumin, cinnamon, ¹⁄₂ teaspoon salt, and jalapeños. Bring to a boil, then reduce heat to low and simmer 1 hour. Allow to cool to room temperature (about 1 hour), strain into a small container, and refrigerate 4 hours up to overnight.

2. Heat olive oil in a large pan. Cook pork belly, turning during cooking so each side is browned and pork is cooked through to 165°F, about 5 minutes.

3. Pour 1¹⁄₂" water into a medium nonstick skillet and begin to heat over medium heat. Line a medium plate with paper towels. Crack each egg into its own small glass bowl.

4. Once water has reached 190°F, use a slotted spoon to lightly stir water and pop bubbles along bottom of pan. Add white wine vinegar and stir to combine. One at a time, push bowls with eggs into hot water and slide eggs into water, then remove bowls. Maintain heat 4 minutes and 30 seconds. Carefully remove eggs with slotted spoon and place on prepared plate. Sprinkle with remaining ¼ teaspoon salt and pepper.
5. Toast brioche and slice into strips.
6. Put pork belly on one side of each of two plates, followed by poached egg, brioche strips, and a dollop of tomato jam on other side. Serve immediately.

EPCOT Park Tip

Be sure to check out the Festival Entertainment offerings while you're at EPCOT. The EPCOT International Festival of the Arts often hosts the popular Disney on Broadway series, where singers from Disney stage productions perform on the America Gardens Theatre stage. Admission is even included in your park ticket!

Steamed Asian Impossible Dumplings

Le Cellier Steakhouse, Canada Pavilion

Asian Impossible Dumplings...from the Canada pavilion? Those who aren't familiar with Canada might be surprised that this dish has no maple syrup or cheese curds, but, in fact, Canada is home to an incredibly diverse world population that includes immigrants from many parts of Asia. This dish is also vegan and contains yummy and healthful vegetables.

SERVES 4

- 2 teaspoons sesame oil
- 1 tablespoon minced fresh ginger
- 3 tablespoons soy sauce
- 2 tablespoons mirin
- 4 cups vegetable stock
- 1 pound Impossible Burger
- 1 cup thinly sliced cabbage
- 1 teaspoon salt
- 1/2 teaspoon ground black pepper
- 20 circular dumpling wrappers
- 16 pieces bok choy
- 5 ounces trimmed green beans
- 1 cup sliced red bell pepper

1. Pour sesame oil into a medium pot over medium-high heat. Add ginger, soy sauce, mirin, and vegetable stock. Bring to a boil, then reduce heat to low and simmer 15–20 minutes until flavors have developed.

2. Mix Impossible Burger, cabbage, salt, and black pepper in a large bowl. Scoop 1 tablespoon filling into center of each dumpling wrapper. Wet a finger and run along outside edge of each wrapper. Bring edges up to the middle to form a pyramid shape.

3. Fill a large pot with 2" water. Bring to a boil over high heat, then reduce heat to low. Place a steamer basket over boiling water and add bok choy, green beans, bell pepper, radishes, and edamame. Steam 3–5 minutes until all vegetables are fork-tender. Divide vegetables into four serving bowls.

(continued on next page)

4 medium radishes,
  sliced
1/2 cup frozen edamame
24 ounces vegetable oil,
  for frying
40 strands stir-fry rice
  noodles, divided
4 fresh basil leaves

4. Replace steamer basket and continue simmering water. Add dumplings to basket and steam in batches 10–15 minutes until all dumplings are cooked. Add 5 dumplings to each serving bowl. Ladle ginger broth into each bowl.

5. In a wide pan over medium heat, heat oil to 375°F. Add 10 rice noodles at a time to flash fry. Noodles will pop up in about 10 seconds into fluffy white curls when done. Use a slotted spoon to carefully remove noodles and place in a serving bowl. Top each bowl with 1 basil leaf. Serve immediately.

Savory Impossible Hot Pot

Rose & Crown Dining Room, United Kingdom Pavilion

"Hot Pot" is otherwise known as "Shepherd's Pie," but this one doesn't have anything shepherded as part of it! That's right: This is a completely meat-free "meat" pie. If you don't like Impossible beef, this recipe can be made exactly the same way, substituting lean ground beef instead.

SERVES 2

4 medium russet potatoes, peeled and cubed
1 pound Impossible Burger
3 teaspoons salt, divided
1$\frac{1}{2}$ teaspoons ground black pepper, divided
1 medium parsnip, peeled and diced
1 large carrot, peeled and diced
$\frac{1}{4}$ cup diced cauliflower
$\frac{1}{4}$ cup diced button mushrooms
$\frac{1}{3}$ cup frozen pearl onions
$\frac{1}{4}$ cup diced green beans
2 tablespoons margarine
$\frac{1}{4}$ cup nondairy whipping cream
1 teaspoon garlic powder
1 tablespoon chopped fresh chives

1. Fill a medium pot with water over medium-high heat. Once water is boiling, add potatoes and boil until fork-tender, 15–20 minutes. Drain.

2. Meanwhile, cook Impossible Burger in a large nonstick pan over medium-high heat 5–8 minutes until cooked through and crumbly. Drain, season with 1 teaspoon salt and $\frac{1}{2}$ teaspoon pepper, and set aside.

3. In the same pan over medium-high heat, add parsnip, carrot, cauliflower, mushrooms, onions, and green beans. Season with 1 teaspoon salt and $\frac{1}{2}$ teaspoon pepper. Cook until fork-tender and bright, about 5 minutes. Set aside.

4. Add margarine to potatoes in pot and stir to melt. Add cream, remaining 1 teaspoon salt and $\frac{1}{2}$ teaspoon pepper, and garlic powder. Mash with a potato masher until very smooth (add more cream if needed). Scoop into a piping bag fitted with a large star tip.

5. Mix together Impossible Burger and vegetables. Smooth into a medium bowl or skillet that perfectly fits filling if piled about 1" thick. Pipe dollops of mashed potatoes onto filling. Sprinkle on chives. Serve immediately. Leftovers can be covered in plastic wrap and refrigerated up to 3 days.

Spicy Pineapple Hot Dogs

Pineapple Promenade, EPCOT International Flower & Garden Festival

The most popular pineapple dish at Disney by far is the Dole Whip. But this savory option just might be a favorite lunch item in your house if you love mixing fruity and spicy flavors together. If spicy isn't your thing, feel free to scale back the sriracha as much as you need to get to the heat level you're comfortable with. Alternately, if you *love* spice, add a little more!

SERVES 2

For Pineapple Chutney

1 cup pineapple tidbits
$1/2$ small yellow onion, peeled and diced
$1/2$ cup pure honey
$1/4$ cup apple cider vinegar
2 teaspoons curry powder
$1/2$ teaspoon minced fresh ginger
2 teaspoons sriracha
$1/2$ teaspoon salt

For Hot Dogs

2 cooked beef frank hot dogs
2 hot dog buns
$1/4$ cup mayonnaise
1 tablespoon sriracha
2 tablespoons crushed plantain chips

1. To make Pineapple Chutney: In a small saucepan over medium-high heat, combine pineapple, onion, honey, apple cider vinegar, curry powder, ginger, sriracha, and salt. Bring to a boil, then reduce heat to low and simmer 30 minutes. Remove from heat and set aside.

2. To make Hot Dogs: Place 1 warmed hot dog into each bun. Scoop Pineapple Chutney on top. Combine mayonnaise and sriracha in small bowl and drizzle onto Hot Dogs. Top with crushed plantain chips and serve immediately.

Potato Pancakes with Applesauce

Bauernmarkt: Farmer's Market, EPCOT International Flower & Garden Festival

Applesauce is very easy to locate in a grocery store and is typically low cost. You'll find with this recipe that it is also very easy to make at home and takes only 15 minutes and a handful of affordable ingredients. Whether you decide to use store-bought applesauce or make your own is no matter: Both options are easy and delicious and will perfectly complement these savory potato pancakes.

SERVES 4

For Applesauce

4 small Gala apples, cored, peeled, and diced
1/2 cup granulated sugar
3/4 cup water
1 teaspoon ground cinnamon

For Potato Pancakes

1 tablespoon vegetable oil
1/2 small yellow onion, peeled and diced
2 medium russet potatoes, peeled and shredded
1 tablespoon cornstarch
1/3 cup all-purpose flour
2 tablespoons nondairy whipping cream
1 1/2 teaspoons salt
1/2 teaspoon ground black pepper
1/2 teaspoon baking powder

1. To make Applesauce: Combine all ingredients in a medium saucepan over medium heat. Stir frequently 15 minutes, then remove pan from heat. Mash ingredients with a potato masher to desired consistency. Pour into a large container and refrigerate 2 hours up to overnight.

2. To make Potato Pancakes: Heat oil in a large nonstick skillet over medium-high heat. Line a large plate with paper towels.

3. Combine remaining ingredients in a large bowl. Scoop about 1/4 cup potato mixture into pan and flatten slightly with a spatula to about 1/2" thickness. Once underside is browned, flip Potato Pancakes and cook opposite side (about 2 minutes per side). Cook about four at a time. Transfer to prepared plate once cooked and repeat with remaining mixture.

4. Serve Potato Pancakes with a dollop of Applesauce each.

Seared Verlasso Salmon

Flavor Full Kitchen, EPCOT International Flower & Garden Festival

Let's address the fish in the room: What exactly is Verlasso salmon? It is a premium category of salmon that has a firm texture and mild flavor, and it is sustainably farmed to better secure the health of the fish and the oceans. EPCOT has always been a supporter and educator of sustainability and innovative farming techniques. Guests can see some of these methods while riding the attraction Living with the Land located in World Nature. If you don't have access to Verlasso salmon where you are, you can substitute any fresh salmon available.

SERVES 2

- ¼ cup frozen shelled edamame
- 1 (8.5-ounce) pouch instant farro, cooked according to package instructions
- 1 tablespoon olive oil
- 2 (3-ounce) fillets Verlasso salmon
- 1 teaspoon salt
- ½ teaspoon ground black pepper
- ¼ cup microgreens

1. Pour frozen edamame into a medium microwave-safe bowl and microwave on high 1 minute or until warmed through. Add farro to edamame and mix to combine. Set aside.
2. Heat olive oil in a large nonstick skillet over medium-high heat. Season salmon with salt and pepper. Add salmon skin-side down to pan and cook 8 minutes, flipping halfway through cooking, until fish is fork-tender and internal temperature reaches 125°F–130°F.
3. Scoop ½ cup farro mixture onto two serving plates. Place salmon on top of farro and top fillets with microgreens. Serve immediately.

EPCOT Park Tip

If you love Living with the Land as much as I do, you'll want to check out the special Behind the Seeds tour, which offers a close-up look at how farmers and scientists create and use those amazing EPCOT growing techniques.

Crispy Pork Belly with Black Beans and Tomato

Brazil, EPCOT International Food & Wine Festival

This simple yet satisfying dish can be enjoyed at the Brazil booth at the EPCOT International Food & Wine Festival—and now year-round at home! Though not a permanent location at EPCOT yet, Brazil is one of the most discussed fan-favorite country when it comes to possible future pavilions at the park.

SERVES 2

½ (16-ounce) can refried black beans
2 teaspoons salt, divided
1 teaspoon ground black pepper, divided
1 tablespoon vegetable oil
2 (2" × 3") chunks pork belly
2 tablespoons diced red onion
¼ cup diced Roma tomatoes
1 tablespoon microgreens

1. Scoop black beans into a small microwave-safe bowl and heat on high in 30-second increments, stirring between cook times, until warmed through. Stir in 1 teaspoon salt and ½ teaspoon pepper. Set aside.
2. Heat oil in a large nonstick skillet over medium heat. Season pork belly with remaining salt and pepper on all sides. Once pan is hot, add pork and cook, turning frequently, until all sides are browned and internal temperature reaches 165°F, about 5–8 minutes. Set aside.
3. Stir together onion and tomatoes in a small bowl.
4. Scoop beans onto two serving plates, then top with pork belly, followed by onion mixture. Sprinkle with microgreens. Serve immediately.

Teriyaki-Glazed SPAM Hash

Hawai'i, EPCOT International Food & Wine Festival

SPAM doesn't have the best reputation. It is typically seen as a meat you might have buried deep in your pantry for emergencies only. However, SPAM has never been out of style in Hawaii. Many local dishes on the islands contain this canned meat, and they are all incredibly tasty! Combined with the starchy potatoes and bright crispy peppers, this makes a well-rounded dish you can enjoy for any meal of the day.

SERVES 2

1 tablespoon vegetable oil
2 large russet potatoes, peeled and cubed
1/2 medium red bell pepper, seeded and diced
1/2 medium green bell pepper, seeded and diced
1/2 medium yellow onion, peeled and diced
1 teaspoon minced fresh garlic
1/2 (12-ounce) can SPAM, cubed
1/2 cup teriyaki sauce
1/4 cup mayonnaise
1 tablespoon sriracha
1 tablespoon diced green onion

1. Heat oil in a large nonstick skillet over medium-high heat. Add potatoes and cook 8–10 minutes, stirring often, until fork-tender.
2. Add bell peppers, onion, garlic, and SPAM cubes to skillet. Stir to combine and cook 2 minutes. Add teriyaki sauce, stir, and cook 2 minutes more.
3. Scoop mixture into two serving bowls. Combine mayonnaise and sriracha in a small bowl and drizzle over hash. Sprinkle with green onion. Serve immediately.

Kielbasa and Potato Pierogi

Wine and Dine featuring Festival Favorites, EPCOT International Food & Wine Festival

Kielbasa is a type of sausage known for flavors of garlic, smoke, cloves, pimentos, and marjoram. It is native to Poland, and Polish people have a distinct nostalgia about roasting these sausages on skewers around a campfire. If you are looking for them at the grocery store, they are almost always packaged in a horseshoe-like shape to be distinguished from the bratwursts and chorizos. The meaty flavor pairs beautifully with the starchy potato pierogi.

SERVES 2

- 2½ cups all-purpose flour
- 1 teaspoon salt
- 1 tablespoon salted butter, melted
- 1 cup plus 1 tablespoon sour cream, divided
- 1 large egg
- 1 large egg yolk
- 2 tablespoons vegetable oil, divided
- 3 large russet potatoes, peeled and cubed
- ½ cup shredded Cheddar cheese
- 1 tablespoon cream cheese, softened

1. In the bowl of a stand mixer, add flour, salt, butter, 1 cup sour cream, egg, egg yolk, and 1 tablespoon oil. Mix until ingredients come together. Switch to dough hook and mix 5 more minutes. Dough should be a bit wet but able to be worked with your hands. Cover bowl with a clean towel and set in a warm place (such as near a stove) to rest 20 minutes.

2. Put potatoes in a large pot and cover with water. Bring to a boil over medium-high heat and cook until fork-tender, 15–20 minutes. Drain and mash. Mix in Cheddar cheese, cream cheese, onion salt, salt, and pepper.

3. Roll out dough to ¼" thick on a floured surface. Use a biscuit cutter or lid about 5" in diameter to cut circles of dough. Place 1 tablespoon potato mixture on center of each circle, fold in half, and crimp around edges with a fork to seal.

(continued on next page)

1 teaspoon onion salt
1 teaspoon salt
$\frac{1}{2}$ teaspoon ground black
pepper
5 slices kielbasa
1 teaspoon diced fresh
chives

4. Refill pot with water and bring to a boil over medium-high heat. Set a large nonstick frying pan over medium-high heat. Line a large plate with paper towels.
5. Working in batches of about 5 pierogi, gently drop into boiling water. When they float, in about 30 seconds, remove with a slotted spoon. Heat remaining 1 tablespoon oil in a medium frying pan over medium heat and add pierogi as they come out of water. Sear each 1–2 minutes per side until browned. Transfer to prepared plate.
6. In same nonstick frying pan, cook kielbasa pieces 3–5 minutes until warmed through. Serve pierogi and kielbasa drizzled with remaining 1 tablespoon sour cream and sprinkled with chives.

Gourmet Macaroni and Cheese with Boursin Garlic & Fine Herbs Cheese topped with Herbed Panko

Mac & Cheese Hosted by Boursin Cheese, EPCOT International Food & Wine Festival

Nothing says comfort food like mac and cheese. This recipe is as deluxe and decadent as they come. The combination of Cheddar cheeses and the creaminess of the Boursin will have you forgetting about the boxed mac and cheese you usually reach for.

SERVES 4

½ pound elbow macaroni
½ cup plus 3 tablespoons salted butter, divided
½ cup all-purpose flour
4 cups whole milk
1 teaspoon garlic powder
1 teaspoon onion powder
4 ounces shredded white Cheddar cheese
4 ounces shredded sharp Cheddar cheese

1. Cook macaroni according to package instructions. Drain and set aside.
2. In a large pot over medium heat, melt ½ cup butter and stir in flour. Cook until golden brown, 2–3 minutes. Add milk, garlic powder, and onion powder and stir to combine. Bring to a boil, stirring often, then reduce heat to low.
3. Add both Cheddar cheeses and 1 package Boursin cheese. Stir until all cheeses are melted. Add salt and pepper, then stir in cooked macaroni.

(continued on next page)

2 (5.2-ounce) containers
  Boursin Garlic & Fine
  Herbs cheese, divided
1 teaspoon salt
1/2 teaspoon ground
  black pepper
1/2 cup plain panko bread
  crumbs

4. Melt remaining 3 tablespoons butter in a small pan over medium heat and add bread crumbs. Toast until medium brown, about 2 minutes. Remove from heat.

5. Scoop macaroni into four small bowls. Slice remaining package Boursin cheese and top each bowl with 1 slice, then sprinkle with toasted bread crumbs. Serve immediately. Leftovers can be stored in a sealed container in the refrigerator up to 4 days.

Serving Suggestion

This could be served as an appetizer by scooping the macaroni into individual cups and topping each cup with some toasted panko bread crumbs and a bit of fresh Boursin cheese.

CHAPTER 5

Desserts

Did you save dessert for after you finished your meal? Or did you flip right to this page? Either way is just fine: This is your food journey around the world, and you can go wherever you please!

In this chapter, every country and primary festival of World Showcase is represented through sweet and unique desserts that you may have never even heard of before. But don't worry about not knowing names or ingredients: Each recipe has been created for beginners and advanced bakers alike. From China's Banana Cheesecake Egg Rolls and Italy's Cannoli to Germany's Milk Chocolate Pecan Turtles and Japan's Mango Mousse Cake, you may just discover your next family staple. Be sure to read all the instructions first before jumping in.

Pastel de Queso con Cajeta

San Angel Inn Restaurante, Mexico Pavilion

Cajeta is a caramel sauce made from goats' milk and can often be found in the Hispanic section of the grocery store. However, if you cannot find cajeta, just sub in any caramel sauce you like. Try using dulce de leche if you have extra from making Dulce de Leche Ice Cream (see recipe in this chapter). The base cheesecake of this dish is classic and delicious, while the sliced almonds add texture and crunch. Add whatever kinds of sliced fruits you like.

SERVES 8

1 ($\frac{1}{4}$-ounce) packet unflavored gelatin

$\frac{1}{2}$ cup granulated sugar

1 cup boiling water

16 ounces cream cheese, softened

1 teaspoon vanilla extract

13 graham crackers

1 tablespoon ground cinnamon

$\frac{1}{2}$ cup salted butter, melted

8 tablespoons sliced almonds

1 cup cajeta caramel sauce

2 cups sliced fresh strawberries

$\frac{1}{2}$ cup fresh blueberries

1. In a small bowl, combine gelatin and sugar. Add boiling water and mix well. Set aside.
2. In the bowl of a stand mixer, add cream cheese and beat on medium speed until soft and creamy. Add vanilla and mix well. Pour in gelatin mixture a little at a time, mixing well between each addition. Refrigerate mixing bowl 30 minutes, stirring every 10 minutes.
3. Grease a 9" pie pan with nonstick cooking spray.
4. Add graham crackers and cinnamon to a blender or food processor. Pulse until mixture resembles fine crumbs. Add butter and pulse until well combined. Pour out into prepared pie pan and use the flat bottom of a glass to press crumbs into the bottom and sides of pan.
5. Pour chilled cream cheese mixture into crust and return pan to refrigerator 3 hours to solidify.
6. Slice cheesecake into eight equal portions. Plate and drizzle each with 2 tablespoons cajeta sauce. Sprinkle with almonds and place strawberries and blueberries on the side. Leftovers can be covered in plastic wrap and refrigerated up to 3 days.

Dulce de Leche Ice Cream

San Angel Inn Restaurante, Mexico Pavilion

Dulce de leche is a delectable Mexican caramel sauce that can sometimes be hard to find but is easy to make. Simply get a 14-ounce can of sweetened condensed milk and place it in a saucepan. Fill the saucepan with water up to ½" below the can's lip. Bring water to a boil over medium heat, then cover pan, reduce heat, and simmer for 2½ hours. Carefully remove the hot can with tongs and allow to cool to room temperature. Open the can and inside is incredible dulce de leche!

SERVES 4

2 cups whole milk
1 cup heavy whipping
  cream
½ teaspoon vanilla
  extract
1 (13.4-ounce) can dulce
  de leche, divided

1. In a large microwave-safe bowl, combine milk, cream, and vanilla. Microwave on high 3 minutes, stirring after each minute. Remove from microwave and stir in most of dulce de leche, reserving about ¼ cup.

2. Pour mixture into an ice cream machine and run about 25 minutes or until ice cream starts to solidify. Scoop one-third of ice cream into a large freezer-safe container in a single layer. Drizzle half of remaining dulce de leche onto ice cream. Scoop another one-third of ice cream into container and smooth out. Drizzle remaining dulce de leche onto ice cream. Scoop remaining ice cream into container and smooth out. Cover and freeze until solid, about 3 hours up to overnight.

3. Scoop ice cream into four small bowls and serve. Leftover ice cream can be stored in the freezer up to 1 week.

Mix It Up!

If you can't find dulce de leche at the grocery store and don't want to take the hours to make it, you can substitute butterscotch or caramel sauce. Both have a similar flavor profile and are typically easier to find in the ice cream toppings section of your local store.

Verden's Beste Kake

Kringla Bakeri Og Kafe, Norway Pavilion

Verden's Beste Kake translates into English as "World's Best Cake." Norwegians often bake this cake on May 17 to celebrate the day their constitution was signed in 1814, separating them from Sweden as an independent nation. Unlike most cakes, this one is baked with the cake batter *and* toppings together! The result is a soft, spongy cake with a slightly crisp meringue top. It may very well be the World's Best Cake!

SERVES 4

3/4 cup salted butter, softened

2 cups granulated sugar, divided

1½ cups all-purpose flour

1 teaspoon baking powder

5 large eggs, separated

1/3 plus 1¾ cups whole milk, divided

½ cup sliced almonds

1 (3.4-ounce) box instant vanilla pudding

1. Preheat oven to 350°F. Line a half baking sheet with parchment paper.
2. In the bowl of a stand mixer, beat butter and 1 cup sugar. Add flour and baking powder. Mix to combine. Add egg yolks and 1/3 cup milk. Beat until well combined and smooth.
3. Spread batter in a ½"-thick layer on prepared baking sheet in the shape of a rectangle. Do not go all the way to the sheet edges.
4. In clean bowl of stand mixer fitted with whisk attachment, whisk egg whites and remaining 1 cup sugar until stiff peaks form, about 5 minutes. Spread on top of cake batter and smooth with knife or offset spatula. Sprinkle almonds over one half (horizontal) of batter.
5. Bake 35–45 minutes until a knife inserted in center comes out clean. Allow to cool, about 30 minutes.
6. In a medium bowl, mix together instant vanilla pudding and remaining 1¾ cups milk. Refrigerate 5 minutes to set.
7. Cut cake in half along almond divide. Spread vanilla pudding over meringue half without almonds. Carefully lift other half of cake onto pudding, keeping meringue and almonds on top. Slice into four large pieces and serve immediately.

Rice Cream

Kringla Bakeri Og Kafe, Norway Pavilion

Rice Cream (or *Riskrem* in Norwegian) is a traditional Christmas dessert in Norway. Sometimes people like to boil a cinnamon stick in the rice to add a little yuletide flavor to the mix. The simple flavors of this dessert will please every member of your family and could even become a new holiday tradition for you!

SERVES 4

½ pound short-grain rice
3 cups water
2 cups whole milk
1 cup hulled and quartered fresh strawberries
½ cup plus 1 tablespoon granulated sugar, divided
1 tablespoon lemon juice
1 cup whipping cream
1 teaspoon vanilla extract

1. Pour rice into a large pot and add water. Cover and cook over medium heat 15 minutes or until water is absorbed.
2. Add milk, stir, cover, and cook 15 minutes more or until milk is absorbed and rice is thick and sticky. Refrigerate 2 hours.
3. In a small saucepan over medium heat, add strawberries, ½ cup sugar, and lemon juice. Mash ingredients with a potato masher and stir until mixture starts to boil, about 5 minutes. Remove from heat and refrigerate 2 hours.
4. In the bowl of a stand mixer fitted with whisk attachment, whip cream, remaining 1 tablespoon sugar, and vanilla until stiff peaks form, about 5 minutes. Change to dough hook, add in chilled rice, and stir to combine.
5. Scoop rice mixture into four small cups and top each with 2 tablespoons strawberry topping. Serve. Leftovers can be stored in the refrigerator up to 3 days.

Mix It Up!

Try using different fruits to make the topping; sub in 1 cup of berries, peaches, oranges—whatever sounds good to you. It is always fun to mix it up in the kitchen!

Banana Cheesecake Egg Rolls

Nine Dragons Restaurant, China Pavilion

This dessert can be made very quickly, and the sweetness of the cheesecake and fruity notes of the banana complement almost any meal! See Chapter 2 for tips on deep-frying.

YIELDS 6 ROLLS

48 ounces vegetable oil, for frying
6 egg roll wrappers
6 tablespoons no-bake cheesecake filling
3 large ripe bananas, peeled and halved
3 tablespoons caramel sauce

1. In a large pot, heat oil over medium-high heat to 375°F. Line a large plate with paper towels.

2. Lay out 1 egg roll wrapper with one point facing toward you. Spread 1 tablespoon cheesecake filling in center of wrapper and lay 1 banana half on cheesecake filling. Dip your finger in water and run along edges of wrapper. Fold point nearest to you over top of banana, fold in sides, and roll together. Repeat with remaining wrappers and fillings.

3. Gently lower 3 egg rolls into hot oil and allow to cook until golden brown, turning frequently, 2–4 minutes. Transfer to prepared plate and repeat with remaining rolls.

4. Place 2 egg rolls on each serving plate and drizzle with caramel sauce. Serve immediately.

Caramel Apple Oatmeal Cookie with Pecans

Karamell-Küche, Germany Pavilion

Soft, chewy, sweet, and salty: These cookies have it all! This recipe is great to make the night before an event where you need to bring a dessert to share. If you want to freshen them up a bit before eating, just pop them in the microwave for 30 seconds or a warm oven for a few minutes to soften the caramels again.

YIELDS 10 COOKIES

- 1 cup salted butter, softened
- 1 cup granulated sugar
- 1 cup light brown sugar
- 2 large eggs
- 1 teaspoon vanilla extract
- 2 cups all-purpose flour
- 1 teaspoon baking soda
- 1 teaspoon salt
- ½ teaspoon ground cinnamon
- ¼ teaspoon ground nutmeg
- ¼ teaspoon ground allspice
- 3 cups rolled oats
- 1 (2.22-ounce) bag Werther's Original Soft Caramels, each piece unwrapped and cut into sixths
- ⅓ cup diced soft dried apples
- ⅓ cup chopped pecans

1. Preheat oven to 350°F and line a baking sheet with parchment paper.
2. In the bowl of a stand mixer, cream together butter and sugars. Add eggs, vanilla, flour, baking soda, salt, cinnamon, nutmeg, and allspice. Mix until well combined. Add oats and mix 1 minute. Add caramels and mix 1 minute. Add apples and pecans and mix until well combined.
3. Scoop 2 tablespoonfuls dough onto prepared baking sheet, leaving 1" between cookies. Bake 12–14 minutes until golden brown. Allow to cool on sheet 10 minutes before serving. Store leftovers in an airtight container at room temperature up to 1 week.

EPCOT Park Tip

Most foods served at a theme park have to be consumed immediately or they aren't very fresh later. However, this is a great treat to take home. You can get a box to go and enjoy them later that night, or even take them back home for family and friends who didn't get to come along on the trip!

Zeppole

It seems like every country and culture across the globe makes their own version of the doughnut. Zeppole are an Italian style of doughnut that come in the shape of little balls and contain ricotta cheese. Despite the ricotta, these do not have a cheesy taste. In fact, you can barely tell there is cheese at all. Instead, the ricotta lends its silky-smooth texture to give a thickness and fullness to the doughnut, unlike the airiness of a yeast donut.

SERVES 3

48 ounces vegetable oil, for frying
1 cup all-purpose flour
2 teaspoons baking powder
½ teaspoon salt
2 teaspoons granulated sugar
2 large eggs
1 cup ricotta cheese
½ teaspoon vanilla extract
2 tablespoons confectioners' sugar

1. Heat oil in a large pot over medium-high heat to 375°F. Line a large plate with paper towels.
2. In a medium bowl, mix flour, baking powder, salt, granulated sugar, eggs, ricotta, and vanilla.
3. Dip a medium cookie scoop into hot oil, then scoop dough from bowl and gently drop 3–4 balls into hot oil. Fry 2–4 minutes until golden brown. Repeat with remaining dough. Transfer to prepared plate.
4. Place 3 balls on each of three serving plates and dust with confectioners' sugar. Serve hot.

Milk Chocolate Pecan Turtles

Karamell-Küche, Germany Pavilion

The key to this recipe is to get the caramel to "firm-ball" stage, or else you'll be left with caramel that is too sticky. Just follow these steps carefully and be sure to have a good candy thermometer in your kitchen arsenal. If you want to mix things up, try different nuts on the bottom instead of the pecans, like walnuts, peanuts, or even macadamia nuts!

YIELDS ABOUT 6 TURTLES

1½ cups whole pecans
¼ cup salted butter
½ cup light brown sugar
¼ cup corn syrup
4 ounces sweetened condensed milk
½ teaspoon vanilla extract
¾ cup milk chocolate chips
1 teaspoon coconut oil

1. Line a baking sheet with parchment paper, draw 3" circles evenly across paper with a pencil, and flip paper over. Spray paper with nonstick cooking oil. Lay pecans in a single layer within each circle. Set aside.
2. In a medium saucepan over medium heat, add butter, brown sugar, and corn syrup. Bring to a boil and add sweetened condensed milk and vanilla. Maintain heat, stirring frequently, until mixture reaches 245°F.
3. Carefully spoon caramel into center of each circle on top of pecans. Allow to set, about 45 minutes.
4. Pour chocolate chips and coconut oil into a small microwave-safe bowl and microwave on high in 30-second increments, stirring between cook times, until chips just melt. Spoon chocolate onto center of caramels and smooth into circles. Allow to set 1 hour before serving. Leftovers can be stored in an airtight container at room temperature up to 5 days.

Cannoli Al Cioccolato

Gelateria Toscana, Italy Pavilion

Most likely, cannoli tubes are not an item in your kitchen. Never fear; online shopping is here! Look for "cannoli tubes" online: They are thin silver metal tubes used to wrap cannoli dough around while the shells are frying. For an affordable price, you can have an item in your kitchen that will create a special and unique dish whenever you want it.

YIELDS 8 CANNOLI

For Cannoli Shells

3 cups all-purpose flour
1/4 cup granulated sugar
1 teaspoon ground cinnamon
3 tablespoons shortening
1 large egg
1 large egg yolk
1/2 cup grape juice
1 tablespoon apple cider vinegar
2 tablespoons water
48 ounces vegetable oil, for frying

1. To make Cannoli Shells: In the bowl of a stand mixer, add flour, sugar, and cinnamon and mix on low. Add shortening 1 tablespoon at a time while continuing to mix on low. While still mixing, add egg and egg yolk, grape juice, apple cider vinegar, and water. Mix until dough just comes together and all flour is combined. Cover with a towel and let rest 15 minutes.

2. Heat oil in a large pot over medium heat to 375°F. Line a large plate with paper towels.

3. Roll out dough to a rectangle about 1/8" thick. Measure length of your cannoli tubes and cut circles in dough with a diameter that matches tube length. Wrap dough circles around cannoli tubes, then gently lower one tube into oil and fry about 1–3 minutes until dough is golden brown. Remove from oil with tongs and carefully separate tube from cannoli shell. Place on prepared plate to cool, about 10 minutes. Repeat with remaining cannoli dough.

(continued on next page)

For Filling

2 cups ricotta cheese
$1\frac{1}{4}$ cups confectioners'
   sugar, divided
$\frac{1}{4}$ cup heavy whipping
   cream
Zest of 1 medium orange
$\frac{1}{2}$ cup mini milk
   chocolate chips

4. To make Filling: In clean bowl of stand mixer, whip ricotta and 1 cup sugar together until light and fluffy. Scoop mixture into a large bowl and wipe out mixer bowl.

5. In stand mixer bowl, add cream and whip until stiff peaks form, about 5 minutes. Fold whipped cream into ricotta mixture and mix in orange zest and chocolate chips.

6. Scoop Filling into a large piping bag and carefully pipe filling into both sides of cooled cannoli shells. Dust cannoli with remaining $\frac{1}{4}$ cup sugar, then serve.

Mocha Tiramisù

Tutto Italia Ristorante, Italy Pavilion

Tiramisù is now a common dessert on Italian restaurant menus, but it really has only existed since the 1960s. Different regions of Italy argue over who exactly invented it and where, but the first recipe didn't hit publication until 1980 and wasn't translated into English until 1982. No matter where it began, this treat is creamy, unique, and super easy to make. It is a no-bake dessert and can be made a day ahead!

SERVES 9

- 2 cups heavy whipping cream
- 1/3 cup granulated sugar
- 1 teaspoon vanilla extract
- 1 (8-ounce) container mascarpone cheese, softened
- 1 (17.6-ounce) package ladyfingers
- 2 cups coffee or coffee substitute, chilled
- 2 tablespoons cocoa powder

1. In the bowl of a stand mixer, whisk cream 2 minutes. Add sugar and vanilla and continue to whisk until stiff peaks form, about 5 minutes. Fold in mascarpone until combined. Set aside.
2. Grease an 8" × 8" glass dish with nonstick cooking spray. Briefly dip ladyfingers in coffee or coffee substitute and lay in a single layer on bottom of dish. Scoop half of mascarpone mixture onto ladyfingers and smooth out. Repeat with another layer of dipped ladyfingers and remaining mascarpone mixture. Dust cocoa powder in a fine layer over top.
3. Cover and refrigerate 4 hours up to overnight before slicing and serving.

Mix It Up!

Don't have any coffee around? Try making this with hot chocolate instead! The flavor will be sweeter and give a whole new dimension to your typical tiramisù.

Coppa Delizia

Gelateria Toscana, Italy Pavilion

Coppa Delizia translates from Italian into English as "Cup of Delight." And delightful it is! Three flavors of ice cream stack together with strawberries and strawberry syrup and are finished with a pile of silky whipped cream. The Disney version comes served with vanilla, cookies and cream, and strawberry ice creams, but in your home you can use whatever flavors you want. And if you're feeling particularly ambitious, you can make the ice cream yourself.

SERVES 1

¼ cup vanilla bean ice cream
¼ cup cookies and cream ice cream
¼ cup strawberry ice cream
1 fresh strawberry, hulled and sliced
2 tablespoons strawberry syrup
½ cup canned whipped cream

Scoop ice creams into a large float cup. Place sliced strawberries around inside of rim. Drizzle with strawberry syrup and top with a swirl of whipped cream. Enjoy with a spoon.

Cookies 'n Cream Funnel Cakes

Funnel Cakes, The American Adventure Pavilion

Like churros, funnel cakes are endlessly customizable, and Disney takes advantage of that as much as they can! This variety includes a slab of ice cream, an effect that is achieved by slicing straight through the paper of a carton of ice cream. If you're not ready to sacrifice a 1/2-gallon container of ice cream for this treat, a regular scoop of ice cream will do.

SERVES 4

48 ounces vegetable oil, for frying
1 1/2 cups whole milk
2 large eggs
2 cups all-purpose flour
1 tablespoon baking powder
2 teaspoons ground cinnamon
1/2 teaspoon salt
1/2 cup confectioners' sugar
1/4 cup chocolate sandwich cookie crumbles
4 (1"-thick) slices vanilla ice cream
1/4 cup chocolate sauce
4 chocolate sandwich cookies

1. Heat oil in a large pot over medium-high heat to 375°F. Line a large plate with paper towels.
2. In a large bowl, whisk together milk and eggs. Whisk in flour, baking powder, cinnamon, and salt. Batter should be slightly thinner than pancake batter.
3. Add 1/2 cup batter to a funnel (or spouted measuring cup), keeping narrow end closed. Starting in the center of oil, pour batter slowly from narrow end while spiraling outward. Cook 3 minutes per side or until golden brown. Transfer to prepared plate and repeat with remaining batter.
4. Place 1 funnel cake on each of four serving plates. Generously sprinkle each with sugar, followed by cookie crumbles. Then top each with 1 ice cream slice, drizzle with chocolate sauce, and place 1 sandwich cookie on top. Serve immediately.

Banana Pudding

Regal Eagle Smokehouse, The American Adventure Pavilion

Banana pudding is often served at barbecue joints across the American South as a light flavor to break up the heaviness of meat dishes. At the end of a rich meal, nothing could be better than a sweet cup of banana pudding. For a fresh variation on this recipe, try adding banana slices to the center between the vanilla wafers.

SERVES 4

1 (14-ounce) can sweetened condensed milk
$1\frac{1}{2}$ cups cold water
1 (5.1-ounce) box instant banana pudding
1 cup whipped topping
3 pasteurized egg whites
$\frac{1}{4}$ cup granulated sugar
24 vanilla wafer cookies
4 tablespoons butterscotch topping

1. In a medium bowl, mix sweetened condensed milk, water, and instant banana pudding. Refrigerate 20 minutes or until thickened. Fold in whipped topping. Set aside in refrigerator.
2. In a separate medium bowl, whip egg whites and sugar until stiff peaks form, about 5 minutes. Set aside.
3. Assemble pudding by scooping $\frac{1}{2}$ cup prepared instant pudding into a 9-ounce plastic cup. Place 4 wafers around inside of cup and add $\frac{1}{2}$ cup more pudding. Pipe on egg white meringue in a zigzagging ribbon over the top of pudding, drizzle with butterscotch topping, and place 2 wafers in meringue standing up. Repeat to make four servings total. Serve immediately.

Tangerine Kakigōri

Kabuki Cafe, Japan Pavilion

Kabuki Cafe is just a small kiosk at the front of the Japan pavilion of EPCOT, but it has been gaining traction as a fan favorite thanks to the cooling and cost-effective Kakigōri. Tangerine Kakigōri has a bold taste, and color to match, without using artificial flavors or colors. Just as it refreshes guests on a hot day at EPCOT, it will thrill your family this summer. You'll be the star of the pool or patio!

SERVES 2

5 tangerines, peeled
½ cup granulated sugar
4 cups shaved ice

1. In a small saucepan over medium heat, add tangerines and sugar. Carefully mash tangerines with potato masher or whisk to extract juices. Continue to stir until mixture starts to bubble, about 5 minutes.
2. Strain mixture into a container, discard solids, seal container, and refrigerate until cold, about 2 hours up to overnight.
3. When ready to serve, divide shaved ice into two serving bowls. Drizzle tangerine syrup over ice and eat immediately. Extra tangerine syrup can be kept in refrigerator up to 1 week.

Cooking Technique

If you don't have a shaved ice machine, cheap hand-crank ones can usually be purchased online. If you would rather not buy one, try blending cubes of ice in a sturdy blender until the ice gets very small and fluffy.

Mango Mousse Cake

Teppan Edo, Japan Pavilion

Each of the three parts of this dish is full of fresh mango flavor. If you can't find mango purée at the grocery store, you can make your own with fresh mangoes. Just dice up ripe mangoes into a blender and pulse until a fine purée forms.

SERVES 8

For Mango Sponge Cake

6 large eggs, separated
1/8 teaspoon cream of tartar
3/4 cup granulated sugar, divided
3 tablespoons vegetable oil
1/4 cup mango purée
1 teaspoon lime juice
1 cup self-rising flour

For Mango Gel

1 cup mango purée
1/4 cup granulated sugar
2 tablespoons water
1 1/2 teaspoons unflavored gelatin

1. To make Mango Sponge Cake: Preheat oven to 325°F. Line two 8" round cake pans with parchment paper.
2. In the bowl of a stand mixer fitted with whisk attachment, whip egg whites, cream of tartar, and 1/4 cup sugar until stiff peaks form, about 5 minutes. Scoop mixture into a large bowl, then clean mixer bowl and return to stand mixer.
3. In stand mixer fitted with mixing attachment, mix egg yolks, remaining 1/2 cup sugar, oil, mango purée, and lime juice until well combined. Add flour slowly while mixing until just combined. Scoop batter into whipped egg white mixture and fold to incorporate. Pour equal amounts into prepared cake pans.
4. Bake 30–45 minutes until a knife inserted in center comes out clean. Let cakes cool completely on a wire cooling rack, about 2 hours. Clean mixer bowl and return to stand mixer.
5. To make Mango Gel: In a small bowl, combine mango purée and sugar. In a separate small microwave-safe bowl, add water and sprinkle with gelatin, then allow to soak 2 minutes. Microwave bowl on high 15 seconds. Pour gelatin water into mango purée mixture and stir to combine.

(continued on next page)

For Mango Mousse

1½ cups whipping cream
¼ cup confectioners'
  sugar
2 cups mango purée
2 tablespoons water
1 (¼-ounce) packet
  unflavored gelatin

For Assembly

24 fresh blueberries
16 tablespoons canned
  whipped cream

6. Line a round plate just smaller than cake pans with parchment paper. Carefully pour gelatin mixture onto plate in an even layer and place in refrigerator 2 hours to solidify.

7. To make Mango Mousse: In stand mixer fitted with whisk attachment, whip cream and sugar until stiff peaks form, about 5 minutes. Fold mango purée into whipped cream.

8. In a small microwave-safe bowl, add water and sprinkle with gelatin, then allow to soak 2 minutes. Microwave bowl on high 15 seconds. Pour gelatin water into whipped cream mixture and stir to combine.

9. To assemble: Place 1 cooled cake round on a large plate. Invert plate with Mango Gel onto cake and remove parchment paper. Place remaining cake onto Mango Gel. Frost top and sides of cake with Mango Mousse.

10. Slice cake into wedges. Add 3 blueberries to each slice in the shape of mouse ears and a mouse head. To serve, add a swirl of canned whipped cream beside each slice. Store leftovers covered in the refrigerator up to 4 days.

Honey Chocolate Baklava

Tangierine Café: Flavors of the Medina, Morocco Pavilion

This baklava is an amazing combination of flavors and textures! Phyllo dough is very thin, and when covered in butter and baked, it becomes crispy and flaky. The nuts and chocolate are almost reminiscent of an ice cream sundae. At EPCOT, you're served just one of these small rolls at a time, but you'll likely have no trouble eating more than one once they are ready at your home.

SERVES 15

3/4 cup confectioners' sugar

1 1/2 cups whole shelled walnuts

1/2 tablespoon ground cinnamon

15 sheets frozen phyllo dough, thawed

1/2 cup salted butter, melted

1/2 cup chocolate sauce, divided

1 cup granulated sugar

1/2 cup room-temperature water

1/4 cup pure honey

1/4 cup sliced almonds

1. Preheat oven to 375°F.
2. In a food processor, add confectioners' sugar, walnuts, and cinnamon. Process until consistency is like pebbles. Set aside.
3. Lay down 1 sheet of phyllo dough on a clean surface. Brush entire surface of dough with a bit of melted butter. Lay down a second sheet of dough on top of first sheet. Brush entire surface with a bit of melted butter. Lay down a third sheet of dough on top of second sheet. Brush entire surface with a bit of melted butter.
4. Sprinkle about one-fifth of walnut filling over dough. Drizzle lightly with 1 tablespoon chocolate sauce. Roll layers up like a tight jelly roll and place in an ungreased 9" × 13" baking pan. Repeat layering and rolling with remaining dough, filling, and chocolate sauce until you have 5 rolls. Retain 1/4 cup chocolate sauce. Drizzle any leftover melted butter on top of rolls.

(continued on next page)

5. Bake rolls until golden brown on top, about 25 minutes.
6. In a small saucepan over medium heat, combine granulated sugar and water. Bring to a boil. Allow to boil 3 minutes, stirring frequently. Remove from heat and stir in honey.
7. Pour honey mixture over still-hot dough rolls. Allow to sit at room temperature until completely cool, 1–2 hours.
8. Remove rolls from pan one at a time and slice each roll into three pieces. Pour remaining chocolate sauce in a straight line down the middle of each roll and sprinkle each roll with almonds. Baklava will keep up to 3 days when covered tightly and stored in the refrigerator.

EPCOT Park Tip

One of the least frequented places in all of EPCOT is the Race Against the Sun exhibit in the Morocco Pavilion. Here guests can learn about how the people of Morocco thrive in the harsh deserts, and you can even test out a driving simulator on how to drive on sand!

Macaron Ice Cream Sandwiches

L'Artisan des Glaces, France Pavilion

Macarons can be fickle little cookies, but don't let that stop you from making them. Make sure your mixing bowl is completely clean and dry, and use a bowl of warm water to bring your eggs up to room temperature quicker. Additionally, don't substitute the almond flour with any other kind of flour! Almond flour is key for macarons, and they won't set with all-purpose flour. This recipe can be customized with your favorite gel colors and ice cream flavors.

YIELDS 6 SANDWICHES

3 large egg whites, at room temperature
¼ teaspoon cream of tartar
¼ cup granulated sugar
1 cup almond flour
1½ cups confectioners' sugar
2 drops red gel food coloring
2 drops blue gel food coloring
3 cups vanilla ice cream

1. Line a baking sheet with parchment paper and set aside.
2. In the bowl of a stand mixer fitted with whisk attachment, whip egg whites on high speed 1 minute, then add cream of tartar. Whip 1 minute, then add granulated sugar and whip until stiff peaks form, about 4 more minutes. Set aside.
3. Into a medium bowl, sift almond flour and confectioners' sugar. Stir to combine. Pour half of mixture into stand mixer bowl and carefully fold in with a spatula. Add remaining flour mixture and fold in until just combined. Scoop equal amounts into two small bowls. Stir red food coloring into one bowl and blue food coloring into the other.

(continued on next page)

4. Add mixtures to two large piping bags. Cut the tip off the bottom or fit with a round tip. Squeeze red circles and blue circles about 3" in diameter on prepared baking sheet, leaving 1/2" between circles, until batter is used up.

5. Firmly tap baking sheet against table or countertop about ten times to settle batter and knock out any bubbles. Let sit at room temperature 45 minutes.

6. Preheat oven to 300°F. Bake 18–20 minutes until barely brown around outside edges.

7. Remove from oven and let cool completely on baking sheet, about 20 minutes. Once macarons are cooled, flip red macaron shells. Scoop about 1/2 cup ice cream onto each red flipped shell and sandwich with a blue shell. Serve immediately.

EPCOT Park Tip

When you visit L'Artisan des Glaces in the France pavilion, you'll notice a large board that lists all the ice cream flavors currently being offered for the Macaron Ice Cream Sandwiches (and other ice cream treats). Try a new flavor each time you visit! You never know when you'll find a hidden gem.

Mousse au Chocolat

Les Halles Boulangerie-Patisserie, France Pavilion

Chocolate Mousse really isn't much to look at, so Disney decided to jazz it up with little crisp pearls that draw the eye away from the brown pile in a cup. Crisp pearls can sometimes be hard to find, but they can be easily replaced with other enhancements. Try rainbow sprinkles, cherries, or whipped cream.

SERVES 4

1½ cups heavy whipping cream, divided
1 cup semisweet chocolate chips
4 tablespoons crisp pearl sprinkles

1. Pour ½ cup cream into a medium microwave-safe bowl and microwave on high 1 minute. Add chocolate chips and allow to sit 5 minutes to melt. Whisk until well combined.
2. In the bowl of a stand mixer fitted with whisk attachment, whip remaining 1 cup cream until stiff peaks form, about 5 minutes. Fold into chocolate mixture until combined.
3. Spoon into serving cups and top with crisp pearl sprinkles. Serve immediately.

Sticky Toffee Pudding

Rose & Crown Dining Room, United Kingdom Pavilion

While this dish is widely considered a British classic, the origins are unknown. One theory says that two Canadian air force officers gave the recipe to a hotel proprietor while they were serving overseas in England. No matter where it came from, this dish is creamy, spongy, and delicious. The cake has a texture and flavor very much like a soft cookie.

SERVES 12

For Cakes

2$\frac{1}{2}$ cups chopped dates
1 cup hot water
$\frac{1}{2}$ cup salted butter
1$\frac{3}{4}$ cups granulated sugar
2 large eggs
2 teaspoons baking powder
2 teaspoons baking soda
2 teaspoons vanilla extract
$\frac{1}{2}$ teaspoon salt
2 cups all-purpose flour

For Custard

8 large egg yolks
$\frac{1}{3}$ cup granulated sugar
1 teaspoon vanilla extract
1 cup whole milk
1 cup heavy cream

1. Preheat oven to 325°F. Grease 12 mini-Bundt pans with nonstick cooking spray.
2. To make Cakes: Scoop dates into a small bowl or cup and cover in hot water. Allow to sit 2 minutes.
3. In the bowl of a stand mixer, cream together butter, sugar, and eggs. Add baking powder, baking soda, vanilla, and salt and mix. Add in flour $\frac{1}{2}$ cup at a time while mixing until well combined. Strain and fold in dates.
4. Scoop batter into prepared pans to $\frac{2}{3}$ full. Bake 15–20 minutes until a toothpick inserted in cake center comes out clean. Remove from oven and let sit in pan 20 minutes.
5. To make Custard: In the top of a double boiler, combine egg yolks and sugar. Add vanilla, milk, and cream. Stir continuously until mixture thickens and coats the back of a wooden spoon, about 10–15 minutes. Strain through a sieve and set aside.

For Butter Rum Toffee Sauce

2 tablespoons salted butter
½ cup heavy cream
⅓ cup light brown sugar
1 teaspoon rum extract

6. To make Butter Rum Toffee Sauce: In a small saucepan over medium heat, add butter, cream, and brown sugar. Bring to a boil, remove from heat, and add rum extract. Set aside.

7. To assemble: Spoon ¼ cup Custard into bottom of a shallow bowl. Place 1 Cake on Custard. Pour ¼ cup Butter Rum Toffee Sauce into divot of Cake. Repeat with remaining Cakes, Custard, and Butter Rum Toffee Sauce. Serve immediately.

Maple Crème Brûlée

Le Cellier Steakhouse, Canada Pavilion

In the United States, the maple syrup selection at the grocery store usually consists of a few 100% pure maple syrup brands, and then several brands of "maple table syrup" that typically contain 0% maple and are just flavored with maple extracts. In Canada, they have an entire *section* of the grocery store devoted to maple syrup and offer varieties that have different percentages of pure syrup. For this recipe, use 100% maple syrup.

SERVES 6

For Crème Brûlée

- 2 cups heavy cream
- 1 teaspoon vanilla extract
- 1/2 teaspoon maple extract
- 1 large egg
- 3 large egg yolks
- 1/4 cup pure maple syrup
- 6 teaspoons granulated sugar
- 6 Maple Sugar Cookies

1. Preheat oven to 325°F.
2. To make Crème Brûlée: In a medium saucepan over medium heat, add heavy cream, vanilla, and maple extract. Heat until bubbles start to form around edge of pan, 3–5 minutes. Remove from heat.
3. In a large bowl, whisk together egg, egg yolks, and maple syrup. While continuously mixing, slowly pour hot cream mix into egg mixture. Whisk to combine, then pour through a mesh sieve to remove any egg solids.
4. Place six ramekins in a large baking dish and fill dish with room-temperature water up to nearly the top of ramekins. Pour equal amounts of filling into each ramekin. Carefully slide into oven. Bake 40 minutes or until custard sets with a slight wiggle.
5. Remove ramekins from water and allow to cool at room temperature 30 minutes, then 2 hours in the refrigerator.

(continued on next page)

For Maple Shortbread Cookies

1 cup salted butter, softened
$1/2$ cup granulated sugar
3 tablespoons cornstarch
1 teaspoon maple flavoring
$1^{3/4}$ cups all-purpose flour
Confectioners' sugar

For Maple Whipped Cream

$1/2$ cup heavy whipping cream
1 tablespoon pure maple syrup
$1/4$ teaspoon maple flavoring

For Garnish

6 large fresh raspberries

6. To make Maple Shortbread Cookies: Preheat oven to 325°F. Line two baking sheets with parchment paper and set aside.

7. In the bowl of a stand mixer, cream together butter, sugar, and cornstarch about 2 minutes. Add maple flavoring, mix, then add flour and mix well, about 2 minutes.

8. Smash dough into a $1/2$"-thick disk, wrap in plastic wrap, and refrigerate 45 minutes.

9. On a floured surface, roll out dough to $1/4$" thickness and use cookie cutters to make about twelve 3" maple leaves. Carefully move to prepared baking sheets and bake 18–23 minutes until no longer soft to the touch.

10. Remove from oven and allow to cool on baking sheets 20 minutes. Dust with confectioners' sugar.

11. To make Maple Whipped Cream: In the bowl of a stand mixer, add all ingredients and whip until stiff peaks form, about 5 minutes. Scoop into a piping bag with star tip.

12. When ready to serve, sprinkle each custard with 1 teaspoon sugar, and toast with a kitchen torch.

13. Once caramelized top has cooled, dollop about $1/4$ cup Maple Whipped Cream onto one side of top, lay 1 Maple Shortbread Cookie onto cream, and finish with 1 fresh raspberry. Serve. Leftover Maple Shortbread Cookies can be stored in a sealed container at room temperature up to 5 days.

Maple Popcorn

Popcorn in Canada, Canada Pavilion

Using a paper grocery bag to mix the popcorn is a special method to evenly spread the delicious coating across all the popcorn. Make sure to give vigorous shakes. Grab a friend to help shake and turn on some awesome Canadian tunes to rock out to as you shake it!

SERVES 15

1½ cups granulated sugar
1 cup salted butter
¼ cup pure maple syrup
¼ cup light corn syrup
½ teaspoon salt
1 teaspoon maple flavoring
1 teaspoon vanilla extract
20 cups popped popcorn

1. In a medium saucepan over medium heat, add sugar, butter, maple syrup, corn syrup, and salt. Cook and stir until butter is melted and ingredients are combined, about 3 minutes. Stir occasionally until temperature reaches 300°F. Remove from heat and add maple flavoring and vanilla.

2. Put about half of popped popcorn into a clean large paper grocery bag. Carefully pour about half of maple sauce over popcorn. Add remaining popcorn, then remaining maple sauce.

3. Roll down top of bag. While wearing mitts or using pot holders, shake bag vigorously to coat popcorn. Carefully pour coated popcorn onto wax or parchment paper on countertop and use a rubber spatula to spread evenly and break up large chunks.

4. Let sit about 20 minutes to allow coating to harden. Store leftovers in an airtight container at room temperature up to 1 week.

Pop't Art

Pop Eats!, EPCOT International Festival of the Arts

In America, purchasing a Pop-Tarts is about the easiest thing to do: They are in every grocery store and come in tons of flavors and varieties. And it seems like new flavors are coming out every day! The fun thing about making your own is the chance to make it into a work of _art_. Allow the kids to choose their own frosting colors and drizzle away to their hearts' content.

SERVES 6

1 (17.3-ounce) box puff pastry, thawed
6 tablespoons strawberry jam
1 large egg, beaten
1 cup confectioners' sugar, divided
2 teaspoons heavy cream, divided
1 drop blue gel food coloring
1 drop orange gel food coloring

1. Preheat oven to 400°F. Line a baking sheet with parchment paper.
2. Cut puff pastry into six equal rectangles. Poke holes throughout rectangles with a fork. Spread 2 tablespoons jam onto each of three rectangles, leaving edges clean. Brush egg onto edges of jammed rectangles and place three remaining rectangles on top. Press edges together with a fork. Place on prepared baking sheet.
3. Bake 10–15 minutes until golden brown. Set on a wire cooling rack to cool completely, at least 1 hour.
4. In a small bowl, mix 1/2 cup sugar, 1 teaspoon cream, and blue food coloring. In a separate small bowl, mix remaining sugar, remaining cream, and orange food coloring. Consistency should be thin enough to drizzle; add more cream if too thick. Drizzle blue and orange icing vertically across pastries. Serve immediately.

Passion Fruit Mousse with Dragon Fruit Jam

Vibrante & Vivido Food Studio, EPCOT International Flower & Garden Festival

This recipe isn't hard to make; it just takes a bit of time. Don't be intimidated! The finished product has many fun flavors and textures layered on top of one another to create a truly unique dessert. If you can't find frozen dragon or passion fruit chunks, try your local specialty grocer. Or use fresh, which is great too. Fresh fruit will not have to be frozen before use.

SERVES 6

For Dragon Fruit Jam

1 cup frozen dragon fruit chunks
½ cup granulated sugar
1 teaspoon lime juice

For Passion Fruit Mousse

½ cup frozen passion fruit chunks
2 tablespoons granulated sugar
½ cup white chocolate chips

1. To make Dragon Fruit Jam: Combine all ingredients in a small saucepan over medium heat. Bring to a boil, then reduce heat to low and simmer, stirring occasionally, 20 minutes. Remove from heat and refrigerate, covered, 1 hour.
2. To make Passion Fruit Mousse: Combine passion fruit chunks and sugar in a small saucepan over medium-high heat until mixture begins to boil. Remove from heat and stir in white chocolate chips. Allow to chill in refrigerator 1 hour, then whip with hand or stand mixer until fluffy.
3. Scoop a ¼" layer of Passion Fruit Mousse into bottom of six small rectangular mousse molds. Spread Dragon Fruit Jam onto mousse. Scoop remaining mousse into molds and smooth tops. Freeze, uncovered, 6 hours up to overnight.

For Dragon Fruit Glaze

½ cup frozen dragon fruit chunks
¾ cup granulated sugar
7 ounces sweetened condensed milk
2 cups white chocolate chips
6 speculoos cookies

4. To make Dragon Fruit Glaze: Add dragon fruit chunks, sugar, and sweetened condensed milk to a small saucepan and heat over medium heat until boiling. Mash with potato masher, then blend in blender or with immersion blender until smooth. Pour hot mixture over white chocolate chips and monitor temperature until it reaches 90°F.

5. Carefully remove mousse from molds and place onto speculoos cookies. Place onto a wire cooling rack over a baking sheet. Pour glaze over each mousse in a thin layer. Serve immediately.

Cooking Technique

The key to this beautiful, layered mousse is to allow enough time for the layers to freeze. This sets them still. If you get impatient and don't allow a full freeze, the layers may shift and slide and cause the whole dessert to fall apart.

Freshly Baked Carrot Cake

Hops & Barley, EPCOT International Food & Wine Festival

You know what? Carrots are a vegetable, and vegetables are healthy—so really this is a vegetable side dish instead of a dessert, right? This cake is loaded with all the good stuff that makes cakes irresistible, including a creamy icing you'll want to keep spooning onto your cake.

SERVES 12

For Carrot Cake

1½ cups granulated sugar
½ cup salted butter
½ cup vegetable oil
3 large eggs
2 teaspoons vanilla extract
2 cups all-purpose flour
2 teaspoons baking soda
1 teaspoon baking powder
2 teaspoons ground cinnamon
½ teaspoon ground nutmeg
½ teaspoon salt
2 cups grated carrots
½ cup chopped pecans
½ cup dried cranberries

For Cream Cheese Icing

4 ounces cream cheese, softened
3 tablespoons salted butter, softened
3 cups confectioners' sugar
1½ teaspoons vanilla extract
3 tablespoons whole milk
3 tablespoons heavy cream

1. To make Carrot Cakes: Preheat oven to 350°F. Grease a jumbo muffin tin with nonstick cooking spray.

2. In the bowl of a stand mixer, cream together sugar, butter, oil, eggs, and vanilla. Add flour, baking soda, baking powder, cinnamon, nutmeg, and salt and mix. Fold in carrots, pecans, and cranberries.

3. Scoop batter into jumbo muffin cups, filling each ⅔ full. Bake 18–25 minutes until a knife inserted in center comes out clean. Remove from oven and allow to sit in pan until cooled, about 20 minutes.

4. To make Cream Cheese Icing: In clean bowl of stand mixer, cream together cream cheese, butter, sugar, and vanilla. Slowly add in milk and cream, mixing until desired consistency.

5. Carefully remove Carrot Cakes from pan and spoon Cream Cheese Icing over tops. Serve immediately.

Key Lime Tarts

Festival Favorites, EPCOT International Flower & Garden Festival

Next time you're asked to bring a dessert to a party, try showing up with these! Everyone is sure to be super impressed by your superior taste and style. The individual-sized tarts, the dollops of meringue, and especially the white chocolate decoration take these from basic to exceptional really quickly. The fresh lime really comes through in each bite and complements the buttery crust.

YIELDS 12 TARTS

2 cups fine graham
cracker crumbs
⅓ cup confectioners'
sugar
1 teaspoon salt
⅓ cup salted butter,
melted
4 ounces cream cheese,
softened
4 egg yolks
½ cup fresh-squeezed
and strained key lime
juice
1 cup cream of coconut
2 drops lime green gel
food coloring, divided
2 egg whites
2 tablespoons granulated
sugar
½ cup white chocolate
chips

1. Preheat oven to 350°F.
2. Stir together graham cracker crumbs, confectioners' sugar, salt, and butter in a medium bowl. Press mixture firmly into bottom and sides of each well of twelve small, long tart molds. Bake crust 10 minutes.
3. In the bowl of a stand mixer, whip cream cheese and egg yolks. Add key lime juice, cream of coconut, and 1 drop green gel food coloring and mix well. Spoon filling onto crusts until wells are almost full.
4. Bake 15–20 minutes until centers have a slight but not severe wiggle. Remove from oven and allow to cool completely in molds in refrigerator, 1 hour. Once set, carefully remove tarts from molds.

(continued on next page)

5. In clean bowl of stand mixer, whip egg whites and granulated sugar until stiff peaks form, about 3–5 minutes. Scoop mixture into a large piping bag and pipe a fat ribbon along the top of each tart. Use a kitchen torch to toast meringue.

6. Pour white chocolate chips into a small microwave-safe bowl. Microwave on high 30 seconds, stir, then microwave 30 seconds more until chocolate just melts. Stir in remaining food coloring. Spread to 1-millimeter thickness on a silicone baking sheet and allow to harden at room temperature 15 minutes. Cut into long, skinny rectangles and place one rectangle on top of each tart. Serve immediately.

EPCOT Park Tip

Many guests miss out on the Festival Favorites booth because it is inside the World Showplace pavilion, which is tucked along a walkway between the United Kingdom and Canada pavilions. In the building are several festival booths—and often musical entertainment.

Strawberry Mousse with Chocolate Crisp Pearls

Flavor Full Kitchen, EPCOT International Flower & Garden Festival

The mold that EPCOT uses to create this dessert is a rectangular bar, about 1" wide, 1" deep, and 4" long, with a squiggly "splat" design on top. Because you're making this at home, you can make it in any mold you want!

SERVES 4

½ pound fresh strawberries, hulled and sliced

½ cup granulated sugar

1 cup heavy whipping cream

¼ cup chocolate crisp pearls

1 cup white chocolate chips

4 drops red gel food coloring

4 gummy worms

4 tablespoons chocolate sandwich cookie crumbles

2 fresh strawberries, hulled and quartered

1. Purée sliced strawberries and sugar in a food processor. Set aside.

2. In the bowl of a stand mixer fitted with whisk attachment, whip cream until stiff peaks form, about 5 minutes. Fold strawberry purée into cream. Fold in chocolate crisp pearls. Scoop into small rectangular molds and freeze 6 hours up to overnight.

3. When ready to serve, prepare chocolate coating. In a small microwave-safe bowl, microwave white chocolate on high in 30-second increments, stirring between cook times, until chocolate just melts. Stir in food coloring.

4. Remove mousse from molds and place on a wire cooling rack over a baking sheet. Pour white chocolate over mousse until coated. Garnish each with a gummy worm and serve alongside 1 tablespoon chocolate sandwich cookie crumbles and strawberry quarters. Serve immediately.

Banana Bread
with Mixed Berry Compote

Shimmering Sips, EPCOT International Food & Wine Festival

Folks with dietary restrictions or certain dietary lifestyles look high and low for yummy food options. Disney does a wonderful job of having tons of offerings for a variety of dietary and allergy needs. This entire dish is plant-based and completely vegan! Even if you aren't vegan or dairy intolerant, anyone can enjoy this incredible dessert.

SERVES 8

For Banana Bread

3 large overripe bananas, peeled
1/3 cup vegan butter or margarine, melted
1 1/2 teaspoons baking powder
1/2 teaspoon baking soda
1 teaspoon salt
1 teaspoon vanilla extract
1/3 cup granulated sugar
1 3/4 cups all-purpose flour

For Mixed Berry Compote

1 cup fresh blueberries, divided
1 cup fresh raspberries, divided
1 cup hulled and quartered fresh strawberries, divided
1 tablespoon pulp-free orange juice
1 cup granulated sugar

1. To make Banana Bread: Preheat oven to 350°F. Line a 9" × 5" loaf pan with parchment paper.
2. Place bananas in a stand mixer or medium bowl and mash until soft and mushy. Add butter, baking powder, baking soda, salt, vanilla, and sugar. Mix until well combined. Add flour slowly while mixing until just incorporated. Pour batter into prepared pan.
3. Bake 40–50 minutes until a knife inserted in center comes out clean. Set aside in pan.
4. To make Mixed Berry Compote: In a small saucepan over medium-high heat, add 1/2 cup each of blueberries, raspberries, and strawberries. Add orange juice and sugar. Use a masher or whisk to stir and mash fruit. Once mixture comes to a boil, add remaining fruit and gently stir to incorporate. Remove from heat. Pour through a sieve to remove some of the moisture and set aside.

(continued on next page)

For Whipped Topping

$\frac{1}{2}$ cup aquafaba (garbanzo bean water)

$\frac{1}{8}$ teaspoon cream of tartar

1 teaspoon vanilla extract

$\frac{3}{4}$ cup confectioners' sugar

5. To make Whipped Topping: Pour aquafaba and cream of tartar into clean bowl of stand mixer fitted with whisk attachment and whip until foamy, about 2 minutes. Add vanilla and sugar and whip until soft peaks form, 2–4 minutes.

6. To assemble: Place 1 slice Banana Bread on each of eight serving plates and top with a spoonful of Mixed Berry Compote and a scoop of Whipped Topping. Serve immediately. Leftover Banana Bread can be sealed in a bag at room temperature for 3 days. Mixed Berry Compote can be placed in a sealed container in the refrigerator up to 1 week. Whipped Topping can be stored in a sealed container in the freezer up to 3 days.

Mix It Up!

If you don't have dairy sensitivities, whipped topping, whipped cream, and even ice cream are wonderful garnishes for this dish. However you want to enjoy it, you do you!

Bananas Foster Waffles

Waffles, EPCOT International Food & Wine Festival

The bubbling caramel of this dish smells simply heavenly. It is a simple way to "level up" a family waffle night, especially if you have some ripe bananas you'd like to use before they get too brown.

SERVES 4

¼ cup salted butter
¾ cup light brown sugar
½ teaspoon rum extract
1½ teaspoons vanilla extract
½ teaspoon ground cinnamon
3 large bananas, peeled, sliced lengthwise and then into half-moons
¼ cup chopped walnuts
4 small cooked Belgian waffles
1 cup canned whipped cream

In a medium nonstick saucepan over medium heat, melt butter. Add brown sugar, rum extract, vanilla, and cinnamon. Cook until boiling, stir in bananas and walnuts, and cook 2 minutes more. Pour over waffles on serving plates and top with whipped cream.

CHAPTER 6

Drinks

You've reached the last chapter of your journey around the world of EPCOT. And it's a great one! The really fun thing about making drinks at home is how accessible they are. Most require no equipment, skill, or prior cooking knowledge. It is the easiest way to bring Disney magic into your home!

This chapter includes a number of alcoholic beverages, but you'll also find instructions for making mocktail versions. These drinks can be served either with a meal from the same country or festival, or as a special treat all on their own. Sip a Viking Coffee for a more extraordinary morning, or pair your Tokyo Sunset with Japan's California Rolls (see recipe in Chapter 3). However you decide to indulge, feel free to tweak ingredients to match the flavor profiles you enjoy most.

La Cava Avocado

La Cava del Tequila, Mexico Pavilion

The La Cava Avocado is the most popular drink served inside the Mexico pavilion. Guests can drink a margarita, then ride the Gran Fiesta Tour Starring the Three Caballeros just steps away from the bar! If you celebrate Cinco de Mayo or Taco Tuesday in your home, add this creamy drink to your lineup.

SERVES 1

For Hibiscus Salt

1½ tablespoons salt
1 tablespoon dried
  hibiscus flowers

For Margarita

1 ounce blanco tequila
1 ounce agave syrup
½ ounce lime juice
½ ounce Midori
¼ medium avocado,
  peeled and pitted
½ cup ice cubes
1 teaspoon Hibiscus Salt
1 lime wedge, scored

1. To make Hibiscus Salt: Muddle ingredients together in a small bowl until salt turns purple. Store in a small sealable container at room temperature up to 3 days.
2. To make Margarita: Add all ingredients except Hibiscus Salt and lime wedge to a blender and blend until creamy.
3. Pour Hibiscus Salt into a shallow dish. Run lime wedge around the rim of a large martini glass, dip glass in Hibiscus Salt, and rotate to coat rim. Discard lime wedge.
4. Pour blended drink into rimmed glass.

Make It a Mocktail

To make this drink a mocktail, simply swap out the blanco tequila for 1 ounce of filtered water and remove the Midori. Follow instructions as written.

Horchata

San Angel Inn Restaurante, Mexico Pavilion

This recipe is for Horchata, but you'll notice the first ingredient *is* horchata. Disney used premade horchata to make this cocktail, and you can usually find it in the milk section of your local grocery store. If you can't find it at a store near you, whip up a batch by rinsing 1 cup uncooked white rice, then adding 4 cups water and 2 cinnamon sticks and allowing to soak overnight. Pour into a blender and blend until the rice is well pulverized. Pour through a fine-mesh sieve into a large pitcher and add 4 cups water, 1 (12-ounce) can sweetened condensed milk, 1 (14-ounce) can evaporated milk, ½ cup granulated sugar, and ½ teaspoon vanilla extract. Stir well.

SERVES 1

4 ounces prepared horchata
1½ ounces horchata rum
½ ounce mezcal
½ ounce corn whiskey
1 cinnamon stick
⅛ teaspoon ground cinnamon

Add horchata, horchata rum, mezcal, and corn whiskey to a short-stemmed martini glass. Add ice to fill. Garnish with cinnamon stick and ground cinnamon.

Make It a Mocktail

Add 6 ounces horchata to a short-stemmed martini glass. Add ice to fill, garnish with cinnamon stick, and top with ⅛ teaspoon ground cinnamon.

Viking Coffee

Kringla Bakeri Og Kafe, Norway Pavilion

How do Vikings take their coffee? Do they pull up to the Valhalla Café and order from a barista who has two huge horns coming out of their hat? Or are there trolls that come by to wipe the tables? You might never know how Vikings take their coffee, but now you do know how Disney imagines they do.

SERVES 1

1 ounce Irish cream liqueur
1/2 ounce coffee liqueur
6 ounces iced coffee
1/4 cup canned whipped cream

Add Irish cream liqueur and coffee liqueur to a pint glass filled with ice. Top with coffee and whipped cream.

Make It a Mocktail

Add 1 ounce heavy cream and 1/2 ounce vanilla syrup to a pint glass filled with ice. Top with 6 ounces iced coffee or coffee substitute and 1/4 cup whipped cream.

Mango Gingerita

Joy of Tea, China Pavilion

The Joy of Tea is a cute little kiosk right off the main walkway in the China pavilion. Its convenient location makes it easy to grab a drink (and maybe a couple of egg rolls) even if you aren't making time to explore the entire pavilion. This light and fruity drink will put a pep in your step for the rest of your day!

SERVES 1

8 ounces mango juice
1 ounce vodka
1 ounce white rum
1 ounce ginger syrup

Add all ingredients to a cocktail shaker filled with ice. Shake, then strain into a plastic cup half full of ice.

Make It a Mocktail

Add 8 ounces mango juice and 2 ounces ginger syrup to a cocktail shaker filled with ice. Shake, then strain into a plastic cup half full of ice.

Frozen Red Stag Lemonade

Fife & Drum Tavern, The American Adventure Pavilion

If you are dining at Regal Eagle Smokehouse: Craft Drafts & Barbecue at
The American Adventure pavilion, have one member of your party go buy some
Frozen Red Stag Lemonades from Fife & Drum Tavern. The tart and sweet drink
goes perfectly with rich, savory barbecue. And if you are at home having a barbecue,
what better drink to enjoy with the meats? Guests can blend up their own drinks
and enjoy a unique beverage on a hot day.

SERVES 2

$1\frac{1}{2}$ cups lemonade,
  divided
2 ounces Red Stag by
  Jim Beam (black
  cherry bourbon)

1. Add 1 cup lemonade to an ice cube tray and freeze solid,
   6 hours up to overnight.
2. Add frozen lemonade cubes, remaining lemonade, and
   bourbon to a blender and blend until smooth. Pour into
   two plastic cups and enjoy.

Make It a Mocktail

*Swap out the bourbon for $\frac{1}{2}$ cup of defrosted frozen cherries.
Add to the blender with the lemonade cubes and cold lemonade
and blend until smooth.*

Berry Punch

Regal Eagle Smokehouse, The American Adventure Pavilion

The ingredients in this recipe truly encapsulate the essence of summer. And what better drink to represent the country born on the Fourth of July than this perfect blend of strawberries and blackberries?

SERVES 1

8 ounces white grape juice
1/2 ounce strawberry syrup
1 ounce blackberry syrup
1/2 ounce peach syrup
2 fresh blackberries
1 whole fresh strawberry

1. Add white grape juice and all three syrups into a cocktail shaker half full of ice. Shake until well mixed, then strain into a 16-ounce plastic cup and top with ice until full.
2. Skewer 1 blackberry, then strawberry, then remaining blackberry onto a wooden skewer and place on top of ice.

Tokyo Sunset

Sake Bar, Japan Pavilion

Starting with the cranberry juice on the bottom and adding the remaining juices creates a beautiful effect that truly looks like a sunset. Adding a paper umbrella is an easy way to up the appeal of the drink even more. If you don't have any paper umbrellas around, try spearing some pineapple or peach slices onto a toothpick for a pretty (and tasty!) garnish.

SERVES 1

2 ounces cranberry juice
2 ounces pineapple juice
1½ ounces coconut rum
1 ounce peach schnapps
½ ounce banana liqueur

1. Add cranberry juice to a plastic cup half full with ice.
2. Add pineapple juice, rum, schnapps, and banana liqueur to a cocktail shaker filled with ice. Shake, then strain over cranberry juice to layer colors. Serve with a cocktail straw.

Make It a Mocktail

For a nonalcoholic version, add 2 ounces cranberry juice to plastic cup with ice. Add 2 ounces pineapple juice, 1½ ounces peach juice, 1 ounce coconut water, and ½ teaspoon banana extract to a cocktail shaker filled with ice. Shake, then strain over cranberry juice.

Frozen Citrus–Pomegranate Slushy

Oasis Sweets & Sips, Morocco Pavilion

Oasis Sweets & Sips has a wide array of drinks available; it is tempting to order one of each. This drink is delightfully tart and blends the flavors of citrus and pomegranate in a cooling slush. Pomegranate juice can be expensive, so don't go out and buy a big bottle if you are just making one drink. It often comes in small bottles, so you can pick up just the amount you need!

SERVES 1

½ cup pomegranate juice
1 cup granulated sugar
1 tablespoon lime juice
1 teaspoon lemon juice
3 cups ice cubes

1. In a small saucepan over medium-high heat, stir pomegranate juice and sugar. Bring to a boil, then remove from heat, pour into a container, cover, and refrigerate 2 hours up to overnight.
2. Add pomegranate syrup, lime juice, lemon juice, and ice to a blender. Blend until smooth. Pour into a plastic cup and enjoy.

Serving Suggestion

Disney serves its slushy a little on the chunky side, with larger pieces of ice instead of a smooth, creamy consistency. Since you are in charge of your own blender, make it as smooth or as chunky as you desire!

Orange Cream Shakes

Citrus Blossom, EPCOT International Festival of the Arts

Have you ever been to a mall food court? If so, you've probably seen an Orange Julius location, and at one point or another may have partaken in a cup of the stuff. These Orange Cream Shakes are reminiscent of the flavors and texture of a classic Orange Julius shake. Smooth and creamy, tart and sweet, it is a delicious treat! Try with fresh-squeezed Florida oranges for the full effect.

SERVES 2

3 cups vanilla ice cream
¼ cup pulp-free orange juice

Add ice cream and orange juice to a blender and blend until smooth. Pour into two small plastic cups and serve.

Did You Know?

Orange Cream Shakes have the option of being purchased in a reusable Orange Bird Sipper instead of a standard plastic cup. Orange Bird has been a long-standing mascot at Walt Disney World, representing Florida oranges.

Diabolo Menthe

Chefs de France, France Pavilion

Hailing from France, Diabolo Menthe is a popular bright green drink served in bars and restaurants and is especially preferred by children. Disney serves its mint syrup with lemon-lime soda, making it a twist on the beloved Shirley Temple. In France, the drink is sometimes served with lemonade instead of soda. Give it a try! Which version do you like better?

SERVES 1

8 ounces lemon-lime soda
1½ ounces mint syrup
1 drop green liquid food coloring

Gently mix soda, syrup, and food coloring in a glass wine goblet. Add ice to fill. Add a straw and enjoy immediately.

Grand Marnier Orange Slush

Les Vins des Chefs de France, France Pavilion

One of the most in-demand drinks in EPCOT, the Grand Marnier Orange Slush tastes a lot like an orange Creamsicle. While Les Vins des Chefs de France may have a huge line, this drink can easily be achieved in your kitchen in the blink of an eye. All you need to do is blend all the ingredients! And the kids can join in with the mocktail version.

SERVES 1

- 2 ounces pulp-free orange juice, frozen in an ice cube tray
- 1 ounce orange-flavored vodka
- 1 ounce white rum
- 1 ounce simple syrup
- 1 ounce Grand Marnier
- 2 ounces ice cubes

Add all ingredients to a blender and blend until slushy consistency is reached. Serve in a martini glass.

Make It a Mocktail

Add 4 ounces orange juice frozen in an ice cube tray, 1 ounce simple syrup, and 4 drops orange blossom water to a blender and blend until slushy consistency is reached. Serve in a martini glass.

Leaping Leprechaun

Rose & Crown Pub, United Kingdom Pavilion

The Leaping Leprechaun can be a little pricey but includes a souvenir glass. You can bring the glass home and make this recipe to feel like you are sitting at the Rose & Crown Dining Room while right in your own kitchen!

SERVES 1

1 ounce vodka
½ ounce silver rum
½ ounce Irish whiskey
½ ounce simple syrup
½ ounce lemon juice
½ ounce lime juice
¼ ounce Midori
4 ounces lemon-lime soda
1 orange wedge
1 maraschino cherry

1. Add vodka, rum, whiskey, simple syrup, lemon juice, lime juice, and Midori to a cocktail shaker. Add ice and shake briefly. Strain into a 16-ounce beer stein and add ice to fill. Top with soda.
2. Skewer orange wedge at the peel, and then skewer cherry. Float in drink for garnish.

Make It a Mocktail

Add 1 ounce simple syrup, 1 ounce lemon juice, and 1 ounce lime juice to a cocktail shaker. Add ice, then shake briefly. Strain into a 16-ounce beer stein and add ice to fill. Top with lemon-lime soda. Skewer an orange wedge at the peel, then skewer a maraschino cherry. Float in drink for garnish.

Pimm's Cup

The Pimm's Cup is a popular beverage served in the UK pavilion and often finds itself on guides to "drinking around the world" at EPCOT. And how could it not be included? The arrangement of bright and unique flavors will likely cement itself in your own home repertoire.

SERVES 1

4 cucumber wheels, about ½" thick
½ ounce lemon juice
½ ounce simple syrup
2 ounces Pimm's No. 1 liqueur
6 ounces lemon-lime soda
½ orange wheel
3 maraschino cherries
¼ lemon wheel
2 lime wheel quarters

1. Add cucumber wheels to cocktail shaker and muddle. Add lemon juice, simple syrup, and liqueur to shaker and fill with ice. Shake.
2. Strain into a pint glass, add soda, and top with ice.
3. Garnish with orange half-wheel skewered through one end followed by 1 cherry, then lemon quarter, then another cherry, then the other end of orange half-wheel. With a second skewer, skewer 1 lime quarter, remaining cherry, and remaining lime quarter. Add to glass.

Make It a Mocktail

Simply swap Pimm's No. 1 liqueur for 7 ounces of Sprite, 1 ounce of lemon juice, and 1 ounce of simple syrup. Follow instructions as written.

Stow Away Mary

Refreshment Port, Canada Pavilion

It's not a typo: This drink *does* include stalks of celery, chicken nuggets, cheese-stuffed olives, and cherry tomatoes. It is like a whole buffet of bar snacks right in your drink! It is basically a Bloody Mary that decided to "Stow Away" with everything on the bar top. So if you are getting a hankering for a drink *and* a snack in the middle of the day, you know what to make.

SERVES 2

8 ounces tomato juice
6 dashes Tabasco sauce
4 dashes Worcestershire sauce
1 tablespoon horseradish
½ teaspoon celery salt
½ teaspoon ground black pepper
¼ teaspoon salt
4 ounces vodka
1 ounce lime juice
4 blue cheese-stuffed olives
2 cherry tomatoes
2 stalks celery
4 small cooked chicken nuggets

1. Add tomato juice, Tabasco sauce, Worcestershire sauce, horseradish, celery salt, pepper, and salt to a sealable container. Stir, then refrigerate overnight.
2. Add 2 ounces vodka and ½ ounce lime juice to each of two plastic cups. Top with ice, then gently stir in refrigerated tomato juice mixture.
3. Skewer an olive followed by a cherry tomato and another olive; rest across top of cup. Skewer top half of each celery stalk. Put 2 chicken nuggets onto each celery skewer. Place celery garnishes in cups. Add a straw and enjoy.

Make It a Mocktail

Simply leave out the vodka and follow the recipe as written.

Sipping Chocolate Flight: White, Milk, and Dark Chocolate

The Artist's Table, EPCOT International Festival of the Arts

Perfect for the person who just cannot make up their mind, this recipe comes with three separate cups of three separate flavors of sipping chocolate! If there is one flavor you don't care for, just leave it out! Curl up with these creamy, sweet, rich, and hot cups and a good book for an excellent fall or winter day at home.

SERVES 2

For White Sipping Chocolate

2 cups whole milk
1/2 cup white chocolate chips
1/4 teaspoon vanilla extract
4 tablespoons heavy whipping cream

For Milk Sipping Chocolate

2 cups whole milk
1/2 cup milk chocolate chips
1/2 teaspoon vanilla extract
4 tablespoons heavy whipping cream

For Dark Sipping Chocolate

2 cups whole milk
1 teaspoon granulated sugar
1/4 cup dark chocolate chips
1/8 teaspoon ground cinnamon
4 tablespoons heavy whipping cream

1. To make White Sipping Chocolate: Heat all ingredients except cream in a small saucepan over medium heat. Stir continuously until mixture begins to boil. Remove from heat and pour into two small cups. Finish with 2 tablespoons cream per cup and stir to combine.

2. To make Milk Sipping Chocolate: Heat all ingredients except cream in a small saucepan over medium heat. Stir continuously until mixture begins to boil. Remove from heat and pour into two small cups. Finish with 2 tablespoons cream per cup and stir to combine.

3. To make Dark Sipping Chocolate: Heat all ingredients except cream in a small saucepan over medium heat. Stir continuously until mixture begins to boil. Remove from heat and pour into two small cups. Finish with 2 tablespoons cream per cup and stir to combine.

4. Serve flights immediately.

Honey Peach Shakes

The Honey Bee-stro is a delightful festival booth where all the recipes feature honey. Bees are essential to the continuing health of the planet, so celebrating and protecting them is of utmost importance! These shakes have very subtle tones of honey. The sweetness comes through without being overpowering. In fact, it's so smooth you could probably drink several before you even realized it! Good thing they are nonalcoholic, or you might leave with a buzzzzzz.

SERVES 2

½ cup frozen peach slices
1 tablespoon lemon juice
1 tablespoon pure honey
½ cup granulated sugar
3 cups vanilla ice cream
¼ cup whole milk

1. Combine peaches, lemon juice, honey, and sugar in a small saucepan over medium heat. Stir frequently until boiling, remove from heat, and allow to cool to room temperature, about 1 hour. Pour mixture through a sieve into a container and chill 1 hour.

2. Pour ½ cup chilled syrup into a blender. Add ice cream and milk and blend until smooth. Add more syrup or milk until desired consistency is reached. Pour into two plastic cups. Serve immediately.

Maple Popcorn Shakes

Northern Bloom, EPCOT International Flower & Garden Festival

If you don't have a fresh batch of Maple Popcorn on hand, feel free to substitute store-bought caramel popcorn instead. Or omit it entirely! The choice is up to you. But your Canadian friends are going to be able to tell the difference because they can sniff out a maple product from a mile away. Proceed with caution, eh!

SERVES 2

3 cups vanilla ice cream
¼ cup whole milk
¼ cup pure maple syrup
¼ teaspoon butter extract
2 tablespoons Maple Popcorn (see recipe in Chapter 5)

Add ice cream, milk, maple syrup, and butter extract to a blender and blend until smooth. Pour into two plastic cups and top with Maple Popcorn. Serve immediately.

Froot Loops Shake

EPCOT Sunshine Griddle, EPCOT International Flower & Garden Festival

It seems like cereal-flavored everything is popping up in grocery stores and restaurants alike. Some people love the reminder of their childhood, while others just love the taste. Whatever the reason this shake was first created at EPCOT, it's sure to please.

SERVES 1

1$\frac{1}{4}$ cups Froot Loops cereal, divided
$\frac{1}{2}$ cup whole milk
3 cups vanilla ice cream
4 drops blue gel food coloring

1. Pour 1 cup Froot Loops into a glass or plastic cup. Pour in milk and refrigerate 4 hours.
2. Strain into a blender and discard solids. Add ice cream and food coloring to blender and blend to desired consistency.
3. Pour into a clean glass or plastic cup and top with remaining Froot Loops. Enjoy immediately with a spoon or straw.

Cooking Technique

Creating the Froot Loops milk allows the flavors of the cereal to permeate the drink without having soggy bits of cereal in your milkshake. Genius!

Cookie Butter Worms and Dirt

At the EPCOT International Flower & Garden Festival, you can see beautiful floral displays, learn about innovative cultivating techniques, and sample scrumptious offerings that make you feel like a kid again. This shake is modeled after the classic "worms and dirt" cup, typically served with chocolate pudding as a base. The cookie butter milkshake gives a new twist to the old favorite and may very well be your new go-to dessert!

SERVES 2

3 cups chocolate ice cream
¼ cup whole milk
3 tablespoons cookie butter
2 tablespoons crushed chocolate sandwich cookies
4 gummy worms

Add ice cream, milk, and cookie butter to a blender and blend together. Pour into two small glasses and top with crushed cookies and 2 gummy worms each. Enjoy immediately with a spoon or straw.

Byejoe Punch

China, EPCOT International Food & Wine Festival

Baijiu is a clear liquor often served in China and comes from distilled sorghum or rice. Its origins can be traced all the way back to the Han Dynasty in 200 B.C.! The flavor can be strong, and the drink has a very high alcohol content. Disney decided to add the flavors of coconut, pineapple, and lychee to help curb the potent taste of the baijiu. Add the baijiu in slowly and adjust to your preferred taste level.

SERVES 1

4 ounces coconut water
1½ ounces baijiu
½ ounce pineapple juice
1 ounce lychee purée
    syrup

Add all ingredients to a plastic cup. Add ice to fill. Stir.

Make It a Mocktail

Just leave out the baijiu for an alcohol-free version! You'll still get the same refreshing, fruity taste.

EPCOT
Food and Drink
Locations

Use the following map to discover where you can find each of the recipes in Part 2 in the EPCOT park! You'll find a numbered key following the map, so you can match locations on the map to what dishes and/or drinks are found there, as well as what chapter of this book the recipe for each treat in that location can be found in.

Recipe Map Locations

MEXICO PAVILION

QUESO FUNDIDO *(San Angel Inn Restaurante, Mexico Pavilion, Chapter 3: Appetizers and Snacks)*

GUACAMOLE *(La Hacienda de San Angel, Mexico Pavilion, Chapter 3: Appetizers and Snacks)*

CARNE ASADA *(San Angel Inn Restaurante, Mexico Pavilion, Chapter 4: Entrées)*

MOLE POBLANO *(San Angel Inn Restaurante, Mexico Pavilion, Chapter 4: Entrées)*

PASTEL DE QUESO CON CAJETA *(San Angel Inn Restaurante, Mexico Pavilion, Chapter 5: Desserts)*

DULCHE DE LECHE ICE CREAM *(San Angel Inn Restaurante, Mexico Pavilion, Chapter 5: Desserts)*

LA CAVA AVOCADO *(La Cava del Tequila, Mexico Pavilion, Chapter 6: Drinks)*

HORCHATA *(San Angel Inn Restaurante, Mexico Pavilion, Chapter 6: Drinks)*

NORWAY PAVILION

SCHOOL BREAD *(Kringla Bakeri Og Kafe, Norway Pavilion, Chapter 3: Appetizers and Snacks)*

NORWEGIAN MEATBALLS *(Akershus Royal Banquet Hall, Norway Pavilion, Chapter 4: Entrées)*

VERDEN'S BESTE KAKE *(Kringla Bakeri Og Kafe, Norway Pavilion, Chapter 5: Desserts)*

RICE CREAM *(Kringla Bakeri Og Kafe, Norway Pavilion, Chapter 5: Desserts)*

VIKING COFFEE *(Kringla Bakeri Og Kafe, Norway Pavilion, Chapter 6: Drinks)*

CHINA PAVILION

HOUSE-MADE CRAB AND CHEESE WONTONS *(Shanghai Holiday Kitchen, China Pavilion, Chapter 3: Appetizers and Snacks)*

PORK EGG ROLLS *(Lotus Blossom Café, China Pavilion, Chapter 3: Appetizers and Snacks)*

SALT AND PEPPER SHRIMP WITH SPINACH NOODLES *(Nine Dragons Restaurant, China Pavilion, Chapter 4: Entrées)*

HONEY SESAME CHICKEN *(Nine Dragons Restaurant, China Pavilion, Chapter 4: Entrées)*

BANANA CHEESECAKE EGG ROLLS *(Nine Dragons Restaurant, China Pavilion, Chapter 5: Desserts)*

MANGO GINGERITA *(The Joy of Tea, China Pavilion, Chapter 6: Drinks)*

GERMANY PAVILION

BRATWURSTS *(Sommerfest, Germany Pavilion, Chapter 3: Appetizers and Snacks)*

JUMBO PRETZELS *(Sommerfest, Germany Pavilion, Chapter 3: Appetizers and Snacks)*

SCHNITZEL *(Biergarten Restaurant, Germany Pavilion, Chapter 4: Entrées)*

CARAMEL APPLE OATMEAL COOKIE WITH PECANS *(Karamell-Küche, Germany Pavilion, Chapter 5: Desserts)*

MILK CHOCOLATE PECAN TURTLES *(Karamell-Küche, Germany Pavilion, Chapter 5: Desserts)*

ITALY PAVILION

MOZZARELLA CAPRESE *(Via Napoli, Italy Pavilion, Chapter 3: Appetizers and Snacks)*

CRUNCHY ARANCINI *(Via Napoli, Italy Pavilion, Chapter 3: Appetizers and Snacks)*

MARGHERITA PIZZAS *(Via Napoli, Italy Pavilion, Chapter 4: Entrées)*

CANNOLI AL CIOCCOLATO *(Gelateria Toscana, Italy Pavilion, Chapter 5: Desserts)*

ZEPPOLE *(Gelateria Toscana, Italy Pavilion, Chapter 5: Desserts)*

MOCHA TIRAMISÙ *(Tutto Italia, Italy Pavilion, Chapter 5: Desserts)*

COPPA DELIZIA *(Gelateria Toscana, Italy Pavilion, Chapter 5: Desserts)*

THE AMERICAN ADVENTURE PAVILION

POWER GREENS SALAD *(Regal Eagle Smokehouse, The American Adventure Pavilion, Chapter 3: Appetizers and Snacks)*

SLICED TEXAS BEEF BRISKET SANDWICHES *(Regal Eagle Smokehouse, The American Adventure Pavilion, Chapter 4: Entrées)*

NORTH CAROLINA CHOPPED SMOKED PORK BUTT *(Regal Eagle Smokehouse, The American Adventure Pavilion, Chapter 4: Entrées)*

BBQ JACKFRUIT BURGERS *(Regal Eagle Smokehouse, The American Adventure Pavilion, Chapter 4: Entrées)*

BANANA PUDDING *(Regal Eagle Smokehouse, The American Adventure Pavilion, Chapter 5: Desserts)*

COOKIES 'N CREAM FUNNEL CAKE *(Funnel Cakes, The American Adventure, Chapter 5: Desserts)*

FROZEN RED STAG LEMONADE *(Fife & Drum Tavern, The American Adventure Pavilion, Chapter 6: Drinks)*

BERRY PUNCH *(Regal Eagle Smokehouse, The American Adventure Pavilion, Chapter 6: Drinks)*

JAPAN PAVILION

CALIFORNIA ROLLS *(Kabuki Cafe, Japan Pavilion, Chapter 3: Appetizers and Snacks)*

MENCHI KATSU SLIDERS *(Katsura Grill, Japan Pavilion, Chapter 3: Appetizers and Snacks)*

TONKOTSU (PORK) RAMEN *(Katsura Grill, Japan Pavilion, Chapter 4: Entrées)*

NIHONBASHI *(Teppan Edo, Japan Pavilion, Chapter 4: Entrées)*

TANGERINE KAKIGŌRI *(Kabuki Cafe, Japan Pavilion, Chapter 5: Desserts)*

MANGO MOUSSE CAKE *(Teppan Edo, Japan Pavilion, Chapter 5: Desserts)*

TOKYO SUNSET *(Sake Bar, Japan Pavilion, Chapter 6: Drinks)*

MOROCCO PAVILION

MELOMAKARONA *(Oasis Sweets & Sips, Morocco Pavilion, Chapter 3: Appetizers and Snacks)*

HOUSE-MADE HUMMUS FRIES *(Spice Road Table, Morocco Pavilion, Chapter 3: Appetizers and Snacks)*

POMEGRANATE-CHILI CRISPY CAULIFLOWER *(Spice Road Table, Morocco Pavilion, Chapter 3: Appetizers and Snacks)*

LEMON CHICKEN TAGINE *(Spice Road Table, Morocco Pavilion, Chapter 4: Entrées)*

HONEY CHOCOLATE BAKLAVA *(Tangierine Café, Morocco Pavilion, Chapter 5: Desserts)*

FROZEN CITRUS-POMEGRANATE SLUSHY *(Oasis Sweets & Sips, Morocco Pavilion, Chapter 6: Drinks)*

9

FRANCE PAVILION

SOUP À L'OIGNON GRATINÉE (FRENCH ONION SOUP) *(Chefs de France, France Pavilion, Chapter 3: Appetizers and Snacks)*

PARFAIT AUX FRUITS *(Les Halles Boulangerie-Patisserie, France Pavilion, Chapter 3: Appetizers and Snacks)*

BOEUF BOURGUIGNON *(Chefs de France, France Pavilion, Chapter 4: Entrées)*

MACARON ICE CREAM SANDWICHES *(L'Artisan des Glaces, France Pavilion, Chapter 5: Desserts)*

MOUSSE AU CHOCOLAT *(Les Halles Boulangerie-Patisserie, France Pavilion, Chapter 5: Desserts)*

DIABOLO MENTHE *(Chefs de France, France Pavilion, Chapter 6: Drinks)*

GRAND MARNIER ORANGE SLUSH *(Les Vins des Chefs de France, France Pavilion, Chapter 6: Drinks)*

10

UNITED KINGDOM PAVILION

SCOTCH EGGS *(Rose & Crown Dining Room, United Kingdom Pavilion, Chapter 3: Appetizers and Snacks)*

BUBBLE AND SQUEAK *(Rose & Crown Dining Room, United Kingdom Pavilion, Chapter 3: Appetizers and Snacks)*

FISH AND CHIPS *(Yorkshire County Fish Shop, United Kingdom Pavilion, Chapter 4: Entrées)*

SAVORY IMPOSSIBLE HOT POT *(Rose & Crown Dining Room, United Kingdom Pavilion, Chapter 4: Entrées)*

STICKY TOFFEE PUDDING *(Rose & Crown Dining Room, United Kingdom Pavilion, Chapter 5: Desserts)*

LEAPING LEPRECHAUN *(Rose & Crown Pub, United Kingdom Pavilion, Chapter 6: Drinks)*

PIMM'S CUP *(Rose & Crown Pub, United Kingdom Pavilion, Chapter 6: Drinks)*

11

CANADA PAVILION

LOBSTER POUTINE *(Refreshment Port, Canada Pavilion, Chapter 3: Appetizers and Snacks)*

CANADIAN CHEDDAR CHEESE SOUP *(Le Cellier Steakhouse, Canada Pavilion, Chapter 3: Appetizers and Snacks)*

RIBEYE STEAK, USDA PRIME *(Le Cellier Steakhouse, Canada Pavilion, Chapter 4: Entrées)*

STEAMED ASIAN IMPOSSIBLE DUMPLINGS *(Le Cellier Steakhouse, Canada Pavilion, Chapter 4: Entrées)*

MAPLE CRÈME BRÛLÉE *(Le Cellier Steakhouse, Canada Pavilion, Chapter 5: Desserts)*

MAPLE POPCORN *(Popcorn in Canada, Canada Pavilion, Chapter 5: Desserts)*

STOW AWAY MARY *(Refreshment Port, Canada Pavilion, Chapter 6: Drinks)*

12

EPCOT INTERNATIONAL FESTIVAL OF THE ARTS

TOMATO SOUP WITH FRENCH ONION AND BACON GRILLED CHEESE *(Pop Eats!, EPCOT International Festival of the Arts, Chapter 3: Appetizers and Snacks)*

DECONSTRUCTED BLTS *(The Deconstructed Dish, EPCOT International Festival of the Arts, Chapter 4: Entrées)*

POP'T ART *(Pop Eats!, EPCOT International Festival of the Arts, Chapter 5: Desserts)*

ORANGE CREAM SHAKES *(Citrus Blossom, EPCOT International Festival of the Arts, Chapter 6: Drinks)*

SIPPING CHOCOLATE FLIGHT: WHITE, MILK, AND DARK CHOCOLATE *(The Artist's Table, EPCOT International Festival of the Arts, Chapter 6: Drinks)*

EPCOT INTERNATIONAL FLOWER & GARDEN FESTIVAL

WATERMELON SALAD (Festival Favorites, EPCOT International Flower & Garden Festival, Chapter 3: Appetizers and Snacks)

GRILLED BABY VEGETABLES (Flavor Full Kitchen, EPCOT International Flower & Garden Festival, Chapter 3: Appetizers and Snacks)

GRILLED STREET CORN ON THE COB (Trowel & Trellis, EPCOT International Flower & Garden Festival, Chapter 3: Appetizers and Snacks)

TRI-COLORED TORTELLINI (Primavera Kitchen, EPCOT International Flower & Garden Festival, Chapter 4: Entrées)

SPICY PINEAPPLE HOT DOGS (Pineapple Promenade, EPCOT International Flower & Garden Festival, Chapter 4: Entrées)

POTATO PANCAKES WITH APPLESAUCE (Bauernmarkt: Farmer's Market, EPCOT International Flower & Garden Festival, Chapter 4: Entrées)

SEARED VERLASSO SALMON (Flavor Full Kitchen, EPCOT International Flower & Garden Festival, Chapter 4: Entrées)

PASSION FRUIT MOUSSE WITH DRAGON FRUIT JAM (Vibrante & Vivido Food Studio, EPCOT International Flower & Garden Festival, Chapter 5: Desserts)

KEY LIME TARTS (EPCOT International Flower & Garden Festival, Chapter 5: Desserts)

STRAWBERRY MOUSSE WITH CHOCOLATE CRISP PEARLS (Flavor Full Kitchen, EPCOT International Flower & Garden Festival, Chapter 5: Desserts)

HONEY PEACH SHAKES (The Honey Bee-stro, EPCOT International Flower & Garden Festival)

FROOT LOOPS SHAKE (EPCOT Sunshine Griddle, EPCOT International Flower & Garden Festival, Chapter 6: Drinks)

COOKIE BUTTER WORMS AND DIRT (Flavor Full Kitchen, EPCOT International Flower & Garden Festival, Chapter 6: Drinks)

MAPLE POPCORN SHAKES (Northern Bloom, EPCOT International Flower & Garden Festival, Chapter 6: Drinks)

EPCOT INTERNATIONAL FOOD & WINE FESTIVAL

CRISPY PORK BELLY WITH BLACK BEANS AND TOMATO (Brazil, EPCOT International Food & Wine Festival, Chapter 4: Entrées)

GOURMET MACARONI AND CHEESE WITH BOURSIN GARLIC & FINE HERBS CHEESE TOPPED WITH HERBED PANKO (Mac & Cheese, Hosted by Boursin Cheese, EPCOT International Food & Wine Festival, Chapter 4: Entrées)

TERIYAKI-GLAZED SPAM HASH (Hawai'i, EPCOT International Food & Wine Festival, Chapter 4: Entrées)

KIELBASA AND POTATO PIEROGI (Wine and Dine featuring Festival Favorites, EPCOT International Food & Wine Festival, Chapter 4: Entrées)

FRESHLY BAKED CARROT CAKE (Hops & Barley, EPCOT International Food & Wine Festival, Chapter 5: Desserts)

BANANA BREAD WITH MIXED BERRY COMPOTE (Shimmering Sips, EPCOT International Food & Wine Festival, Chapter 5: Desserts)

BANANAS FOSTER WAFFLES (Waffles, EPCOT International Food & Wine Festival, Chapter 5: Desserts)

BYEJOE PUNCH (China, EPCOT International Food & Wine Festival, Chapter 6: Drinks)

Standard US/Metric Measurement Conversions

VOLUME CONVERSIONS	
US Volume Measure	**Metric Equivalent**
⅛ teaspoon	0.5 milliliter
¼ teaspoon	1 milliliter
½ teaspoon	2 milliliters
1 teaspoon	5 milliliters
½ tablespoon	7 milliliters
1 tablespoon (3 teaspoons)	15 milliliters
2 tablespoons (1 fluid ounce)	30 milliliters
¼ cup (4 tablespoons)	60 milliliters
⅓ cup	90 milliliters
½ cup (4 fluid ounces)	125 milliliters
⅔ cup	160 milliliters
¾ cup (6 fluid ounces)	180 milliliters
1 cup (16 tablespoons)	250 milliliters
1 pint (2 cups)	500 milliliters
1 quart (4 cups)	1 liter (about)

WEIGHT CONVERSIONS

US Weight Measure	Metric Equivalent
½ ounce	15 grams
1 ounce	30 grams
2 ounces	60 grams
3 ounces	85 grams
¼ pound (4 ounces)	115 grams
½ pound (8 ounces)	225 grams
¾ pound (12 ounces)	340 grams
1 pound (16 ounces)	454 grams

OVEN TEMPERATURE CONVERSIONS

Degrees Fahrenheit	Degrees Celsius
200 degrees F	95 degrees C
250 degrees F	120 degrees C
275 degrees F	135 degrees C
300 degrees F	150 degrees C
325 degrees F	160 degrees C
350 degrees F	180 degrees C
375 degrees F	190 degrees C
400 degrees F	205 degrees C
425 degrees F	220 degrees C
450 degrees F	230 degrees C

BAKING PAN SIZES

American	Metric
8 × 1½ inch round baking pan	20 × 4 cm cake tin
9 × 1½ inch round baking pan	23 × 3.5 cm cake tin
11 × 7 × 1½ inch baking pan	28 × 18 × 4 cm baking tin
13 × 9 × 2 inch baking pan	30 × 20 × 5 cm baking tin
2 quart rectangular baking dish	30 × 20 × 3 cm baking tin
15 × 10 × 2 inch baking pan	30 × 25 × 2 cm baking tin (Swiss roll tin)
9 inch pie plate	22 × 4 or 23 × 4 cm pie plate
7 or 8 inch springform pan	18 or 20 cm springform or loose bottom cake tin
9 × 5 × 3 inch loaf pan	23 × 13 × 7 cm or 2 lb narrow loaf or pâté tin
1½ quart casserole	1.5 liter casserole
2 quart casserole	2 liter casserole

Index

House-Made Crab and Cheese Wontons, 52–53

Lobster Poutine, 75

Salt and Pepper Shrimp with Spinach Noodles, 90–91

Seared Verlasso Salmon, 121

Flavor Full Kitchen, 82, 121, 178–79, 213

Flower festival. *See* EPCOT International Flower & Garden Festival

Food coloring, 32

Food festival. *See* EPCOT International Food & Wine Festival

Food processor, 33

France Pavilion, 217, 220

Freshly Baked Carrot Cake, 174

Fries, house-made hummus, 69

Froot Loops Shake, 210–11

Frozen Citrus-Pomegranate Slushy, 196

Frozen Red Stag Lemonade, 191

Frying (deep-frying), electric fryer for, 71

Funnel Cake Stand, 151

Funnel Cake Stand, Cookies 'n Cream Funnel Cakes from, 151

G

Garden festival. *See* EPCOT International Flower & Garden Festival

Gelateria Toscana, 141, 145–46, 149

Germany Pavilion, 216, 218

Glass pan, 33

Gourmet Macaroni and Cheese with Boursin Garlic & Fine Herbs Cheese topped with Herbed Panko, 129–31

Grilled Baby Vegetables, 82

Grilled Street Corn on the Cob, 83

Grill or grill pan, 33

Guacamole, 47

H

Hawaii (EPCOT International Food & Wine Festival), 124–25

Holidays, EPCOT International Festival of the Holidays, 26

The Honey Bee-stro, 208

Honey Chocolate Baklava, 157–59

Honey Peach Shakes, 208

Honey Sesame Chicken, 93

Hops & Barley, 174

Horchata, 188

Hot dogs, spicy pineapple, 118–19

House-Made Crab and Cheese Wontons, 52–53

House-Made Hummus Fries, 69

Hummus fries, 69

I

Ice cream

Cookie Butter Worms and Dirt, 213

Cookies 'n Cream Funnel Cakes, 151

Coppa Delizia, 149

Dulce de Leche Ice Cream, 135

Froot Loops Shake, 210–11

Honey Peach Shakes, 208

Macaron Ice Cream Sandwiches, 161–62

Maple Popcorn Shakes, 209

Orange Cream Shakes, 197

Rice Cream, 138

Ice cream machine, 34

Immersion blender, 34

Impossible Burgers

BBQ Jackfruit Burgers, 105

Savory Impossible Hot Pot, 117

Steamed Asian Impossible Dumplings, 115–16

Irish cream liqueur, in Viking Coffee, 189

Irish whiskey, in Leaping Leprechaun, 201

Italy Pavilion, 216, 219

About the Author

Author photo by Valerie Salin

As a child who grew up in Anaheim Hills, California, Ashley Craft could recite the Star Tours ride by heart and navigate the park without a map, and she fell asleep to the sound of Disneyland fireworks each night in her bedroom. After two internships at Walt Disney World and many, many more visits to the Disney Parks, Ashley is now one of the leading experts on Disneyland and Walt Disney World. Her popular blog, AshleyCrafted.com, is best known for featuring recipes inspired by Disney Park foods to help people re-create that Disney magic right in their own kitchens. Her first book, *The Unofficial Disney Parks Cookbook*, became an instant bestseller. She lives with her husband, Danny; their children, Elliot, Hazel, and Clifford; and their cats, Figaro and Strider. Follow her on *Instagram* at @unofficialtastetester.

THE MAGIC OF DISNEY— IN YOUR KITCHEN!

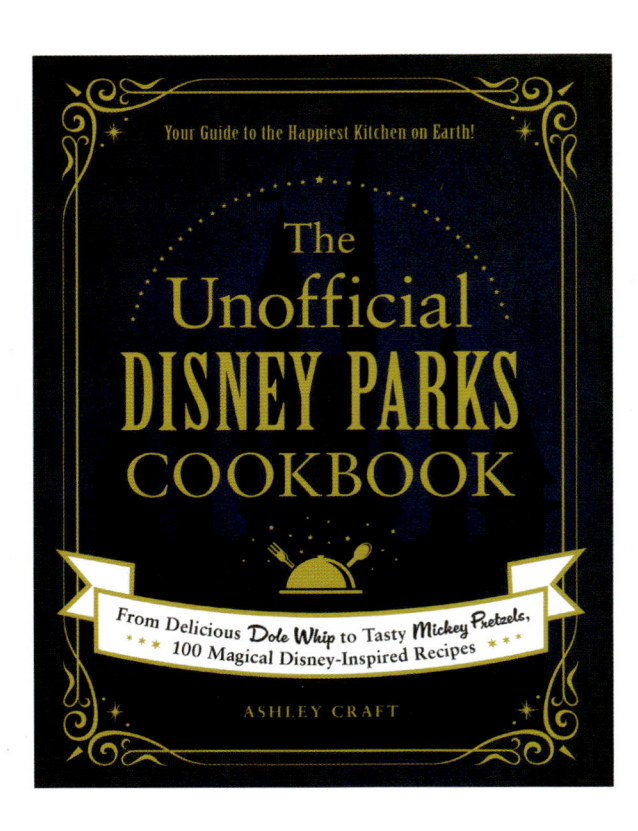

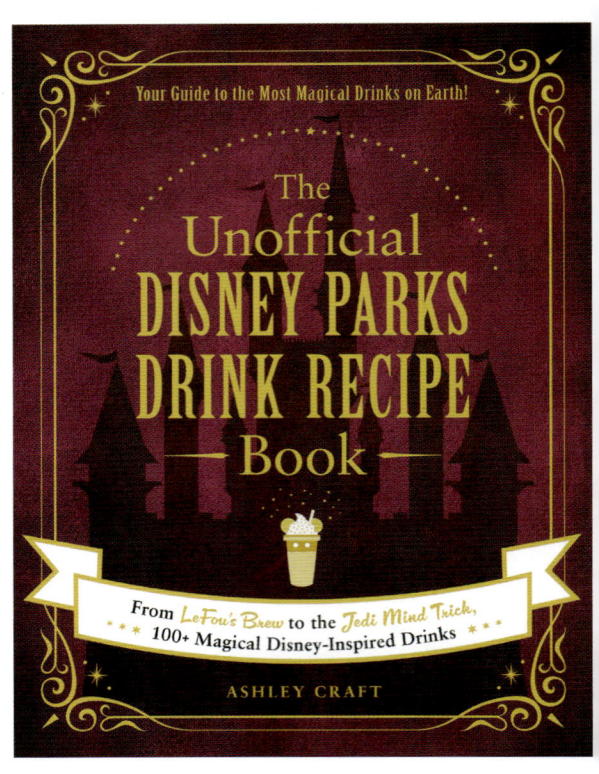

Pick Up or Download Your Copies Today!